INTERNATIONAL DEVELOPMENT IN FOCUS

Leveraging Urbanization to Promote a New Growth Model While Reducing Territorial Disparities in Morocco

Urban and Regional Development
Policy Note

Somik Lall, Ayah Mahgoub, Augustin Maria,
Anastasia Touati, and Jose Luis Acero

© 2019 International Bank for Reconstruction and Development / The World Bank
1818 H Street NW, Washington, DC 20433
Telephone: 202-473-1000; Internet: www.worldbank.org

Some rights reserved

1 2 3 4   22 21 20 19

Books in this series are published to communicate the results of Bank research, analysis, and operational experience with the least possible delay. The extent of language editing varies from book to book.

This work is a product of the staff of The World Bank with external contributions. The findings, interpretations, and conclusions expressed in this work do not necessarily reflect the views of The World Bank, its Board of Executive Directors, or the governments they represent. The World Bank does not guarantee the accuracy of the data included in this work. The boundaries, colors, denominations, and other information shown on any map in this work do not imply any judgment on the part of The World Bank concerning the legal status of any territory or the endorsement or acceptance of such boundaries.

Nothing herein shall constitute or be considered to be a limitation upon or waiver of the privileges and immunities of The World Bank, all of which are specifically reserved.

Rights and Permissions

This work is available under the Creative Commons Attribution 3.0 IGO license (CC BY 3.0 IGO) http://creativecommons.org/licenses/by/3.0/igo. Under the Creative Commons Attribution license, you are free to copy, distribute, transmit, and adapt this work, including for commercial purposes, under the following conditions:

Attribution—Please cite the work as follows: Lall, Somik, Ayah Mahgoub, Augustin Maria, Anastasia Touati, and Jose Luis Acero. 2019. *Leveraging Urbanization to Promote a New Growth Model While Reducing Territorial Disparities in Morocco: Urban and Regional Development Policy Note*. International Development in Focus. Washington, DC: World Bank. doi:10.1596/978-1-4648-1433-4 License: Creative Commons Attribution CC BY 3.0 IGO

Translations—If you create a translation of this work, please add the following disclaimer along with the attribution: *This translation was not created by The World Bank and should not be considered an official World Bank translation. The World Bank shall not be liable for any content or error in this translation.*

Adaptations—If you create an adaptation of this work, please add the following disclaimer along with the attribution: *This is an adaptation of an original work by The World Bank. Views and opinions expressed in the adaptation are the sole responsibility of the author or authors of the adaptation and are not endorsed by The World Bank.*

Third-party content—The World Bank does not necessarily own each component of the content contained within the work. The World Bank therefore does not warrant that the use of any third-party-owned individual component or part contained in the work will not infringe on the rights of those third parties. The risk of claims resulting from such infringement rests solely with you. If you wish to re-use a component of the work, it is your responsibility to determine whether permission is needed for that re-use and to obtain permission from the copyright owner. Examples of components can include, but are not limited to, tables, figures, or images.

All queries on rights and licenses should be addressed to World Bank Publications, The World Bank Group, 1818 H Street NW, Washington, DC 20433, USA; e-mail: pubrights@worldbank.org.

ISBN: 978-1-4648-1433-4
DOI: 10.1596/978-1-4648-1433-4

Cover photo: © Augustin Maria / World Bank. Permission required for reuse.
Cover design: Debra Naylor / Naylor Design Inc.

Contents

Acknowledgments v
About the Authors vii
Executive Summary ix
Abbreviations xvii

CHAPTER 1: Introduction: Well-Managed Urbanization Is Central to Morocco's Development 1

    Urbanization and the delivery of economic and social dividends 4
    How can Morocco's leaders make urbanization work better for shared prosperity? 10
    Notes 11
    References 12

CHAPTER 2: Identifying Key Opportunities for Policy and Investment: Institutions, Infrastructure, and Interventions 13

    Institutions for land management, decentralized service provision, and urban finance: What's next? 14
    Infrastructure needs in cities and regions: What's next? 24
    Notes 31
    References 31

CHAPTER 3: Conclusion 33

    Morocco: Three series of development challenges to overcome for better economic and social inclusion 33
    A favorable context for coordinated reforms at different levels 34
    Three types of targeted public interventions and priority reforms 34
    Reference 36

Boxes

ES.1 Territorial organization: A three-level political-administrative system   xiii
1.1 Urban pattern in Morocco: A city system organized along the Atlantic urban axis   2
1.2 Agglomeration economies   3
2.1 Leveraging information systems to improve municipal revenues in Tanzania   19
2.2 "Contratos plan": An intermunicipal investment mechanism in Colombia   20

2.3 Rationalizing the geography of intermunicipal cooperation: A recent example in France 21
2.4 Morocco's experience with PSP and SDLs 22

Figures

1.1 GDP per capita in countries at 50% urbanization level 5
1.2 Urbanization rate in Morocco, 2000–14 5
1.3 Sectoral shares of employment and value added in the 7 largest Moroccan agglomerations, 10 comparator cities, and 775 cities vs. GDP per capita, 2015 7
1.4 Share of firms in internationally traded and nontradable sectors in select cities in low- and middle-income countries (latest post-2010 data) 8
1.5 Economic growth of Moroccan cities compared with global comparators, 2005–15 8
1.6 Labor productivity in cities in Morocco and in select countries, 2015 9
1.7 Employment as a share of working-age population in cities in Morocco and in select countries, 2015 9
2.1 Growth of built-up areas in Morocco's main agglomerations 15
2.2 Perception of firms in select countries regarding access to land as a major constraint for business development 17
2.3 Access to running water and improved sanitation in Morocco, by region, 2014 18
2.4 Fixed and mobile broadband penetration in Morocco and select Middle East and North African countries, 2015 28

Maps

B1.2.1 Mountains of economic activity in Morocco and Northern Africa 4
2.1 Leapfrog urban development in Morocco: Greater Casablanca and Rabat-Salé-Temara 16
2.2 Physical connectivity for households in relatively sparsely populated regions of Morocco: The case of the Northeast region 27

Tables

2.1 Average commercial speed of buses in Morocco's largest agglomerations 24
2.2 Policy interventions to promote competitive cities in Morocco 30

Acknowledgments

This policy note was prepared by a core team including Somik Lall (lead urban economist), Ayah Mahgoub (senior urban development specialist), Augustin Maria (senior urban development specialist), Anastasia Touati (urban development specialist), and Jose Luis Acero (consultant), with inputs from Andrea Liverani (program leader, task team leader), Abdoul Gadiry Barry (consultant), Olivia D'Aoust (urban economist), Arthur Foch (ICT policy specialist), Herve Hocquard (consultant), Tobias Lechtenfeld (social development specialist), Abdellah Lehzam (consultant), Katie L. McWilliams (geographer), Nabil Samir (transport specialist), Maria Sarraf (lead environment specialist), Michel Savy (consultant), Benjamin Stewart (geographer), Manaf Touati (energy specialist), Olivier Toutain (consultant), and Lamia Zaki (consultant) and collaboration from Thibault Bouëssel du Bourg and Pierre Uginet.

About the Authors

Jose Luis Acero is an urban development consultant at the World Bank. Since joining the Bank in 2013, he has been responsible of coleading and supporting policy dialogue, lending operations, technical assistance, and research activities in the areas of urban development, housing and infrastructure finance, land value capture instruments, city competitiveness, and municipal finances. His country experience includes Argentina, Bolivia, Colombia, Costa Rica, El Salvador, Guatemala, Jordan, Mexico, Morocco, Nicaragua, and Panama.

Relevant research experience at the World Bank includes, among others, being a coeditor of the Central America urbanization review (2017); coauthor of urban policy notes for Costa Rica (2018), Morocco (2016), Colombia (2015), and Bolivia (2014); coauthor of the Jordan housing sector review (2018) and coauthor of a technical note on tax increment financing for Colombia (2016). He holds a master's in public administration in development practice from Columbia University, a master's in economics, and a BSc in industrial engineering from Los Andes University in Colombia.

Somik Lall is the World Bank's global lead on territorial development solutions and its lead economist for urban development in Africa. He heads a World Bank global research program on urbanization and spatial development and founded the Bank's urbanization review program. He is an expert on development policy related to urban and territorial competitiveness, agglomeration and clusters, infrastructure, and impact evaluation, with more than 18 years of experience in Africa, Asia, and Latin America. He was a core member of the team that wrote *World Development Report 2009: Reshaping Economic Geography*; a senior economic counselor to the Indian prime minister's National Transport Development Policy Committee; and the lead author of the World Bank's flagship report *Urbanization Planning, Connecting, and Financing Cities—Now: Priorities for City Leaders*. His work focuses on "place-shaping policies" around cities, clusters, and corridors and the functioning of factor and product markets. He has published dozens of articles in peer-reviewed journals.

Ayah Mahgoub is a senior urban development specialist at the World Bank. She leads urban and territorial development lending and analytical projects in the

Arab Republic of Egypt, Morocco, and Tunisia and in the Middle East and North Africa more broadly. She is also one of the leads of the World Bank knowledge groups on competitive cities and results-based financing. Her current work focuses on urban and territorial development, city competitiveness, intergovernmental fiscal systems and municipal finance, smart cities, and results-based financing. She completed her undergraduate and graduate studies in economics and international development at Harvard University. Prior to joining the World Bank, she worked for the Center for Global Development, Development Innovation Ventures/U.S. Agency for International Development, and the Crown Prince Court of Abu Dhabi. She has worked on urban development in New York City, economic integration of minorities in France, and peace-building initiatives in Sudan as well as on Latin America. She has a BA and an MPA/ID from Harvard University.

Augustin Maria is a senior urban development specialist in the Social, Urban, Rural, and Resilience Global Practice. His current work focuses on municipal management, urban revitalization, and housing and urban resilience in the Maghreb. Since he joined the World Bank in 2008, he has worked in Latin America, the Middle East and North Africa, and South Asia on issues related to urban development, disaster risk management, as well as water supply and sanitation. He graduated as an engineer from the École des Mines in Paris and holds a PhD in economics from Université Paris-Dauphine.

Anastasia Touati is an urban development specialist in the Social, Urban, Rural, and Resilience Global Practice. She leads and contributes to territorial development lending and analytical projects in Morocco and Tunisia and at a global level more broadly. Her current work focuses on urban and transportation planning, municipal management, intergovernmental fiscal systems and municipal finance, and urban economics applied to operational urban planning.

She graduated as a civil and transportation engineer from the École Nationale des Travaux Publics de l'Etat and holds a PhD in urban and regional studies from the École des Ponts ParisTech. Prior to joining the World Bank, she worked for seven years for the French Ministry of Territorial Development, Transport, and Energy, where she led research and operational programs on urban and transportation planning (compact city policies, postsuburban development, and local governance of energy transition). She also worked for the Inter-American Development Bank, leading and contributing to development projects in Haiti (land tenure security, local economic development around industrial zones, and sustainable tourism). As part of her research activities, she has also worked on urban and housing development in Latin America (Chile, Colombia, and Peru).

Executive Summary

LEVERAGING URBANIZATION TO PROMOTE GROWTH WHILE REDUCING TERRITORIAL DISPARITIES

The government program for 2017 clearly states the aspirations of Morocco with regard to both promoting economic growth and fighting against territorial disparities. When considering policy options to pursue these objectives, Moroccan decision makers must consider two major ongoing transformations. The first is Morocco's continuing urbanization process, which has transformed the country over the last decades and will continue to shape Morocco's development given the urban population's expected growth in the decades to come. The second is the institutional reform process introduced through the 2011 Constitution and elaborated through the Advanced Regionalization agenda.

This policy note identifies strategic issues that will arise as well as options that would enable decision makers to reconcile the two objectives of economic growth and spatial equity in the context of Morocco's continuing urbanization, while taking into account the government's ambitious agenda of institutional reforms. This note is aligned with King Mohammed VI's latest call for the implementation of a "new development model likely to respond to all citizens' demands and needs and to keep abreast of changes in the country" (King Mohammed VI 2017).

The main message of this note is that urbanization and spatial equity are not competing objectives when urbanization is supported and managed well. Too often, the concentration of people and economic activities, which characterizes all urbanization processes around the world, is seen as conflicting with the objective of balanced regional development. Public authorities are concerned that rising economic concentration in cities is exacerbating spatial inequalities and often consider options to divert economic and population growth to rural areas. It seems that these worries are unfounded. Indeed, international evidence shows that urbanization and economic development go hand in hand.

Urbanization, when managed well, allows for economies of scale in the provision of services and the development of more efficient labor and product markets, which in turn drive increased productivity. As such, economic growth is inherently "geographically unbalanced." However, disparities in basic living standards are not a necessity. As countries grow richer through urbanization, they can and should aim to equalize living standards and opportunities across their territories. With the right policies, the concentration of economic activity and the convergence of living standards can happen together. The challenge for the Moroccan government is to allow, even encourage, "geographically unbalanced" economic growth, while ensuring inclusive development. These policies should focus on promoting economic integration by bringing lagging and leading places closer in economic terms.

This note identifies priority actions to be taken at national, regional, and local levels to allow public authorities to act within a coherent framework and help urban development to boost economic growth and promote shared prosperity for all.

CITIES: THE KEY TO MOROCCO'S FUTURE

Urbanization continues to transform Morocco's society and its economy. Today 60 percent of Moroccans already reside in urban areas, as opposed to 35 percent in 1970. Although the fertility rate remains higher in rural than in urban areas (2.7 vs. 1.8), rural-urban migration makes Morocco's sustained population growth a predominantly urban phenomenon. According to estimates from the National Statistics Institute (Haut Commissariat au Plan), by 2050, nearly three-quarters of the country's population will be urban. Along with the concentration of people, urbanization will also lead to the increasing concentration of economic activities in cities, which account for an estimated 75 percent of the country's gross domestic product (GDP) and 70 percent of investment at the national level.

Moroccan cities are the engines of today's demographic and economic growth, but they also face persistent challenges. Despite substantial public investments and a strong potential to absorb rural poverty (with poverty rates at 4.8 percent in urban areas compared with 14.5 percent in rural areas), cities remain plagued by important pockets of poverty. In 2014, roughly 325,000 people in urban areas lived below the relative poverty threshold (US$3.1 per day in 2011 purchasing power parity terms) and another 1.6 million Moroccans were economically vulnerable, with higher than average likelihood of falling into poverty when exposed to shocks. Urban unemployment stands at 14 percent, while rural unemployment is 3.8 percent. Youth unemployment, especially, remains an essentially urban phenomenon—at 36 percent vs. 8.4 percent in rural areas (HCP 2013)—and a serious concern.

Persistent spatial disparities are a major cause for concern for citizens as well as for national and local governments. Per capita household consumption is 54 percent lower in rural areas than in urban areas, and uneven access to services and social protection compounds disparities. In recent years, the Moroccan government has adopted ambitious programs to improve living standards in urban and rural areas. Significant improvements in living standards were achieved through national master plans such as the Cities without Slums Program (Programme Villes sans Bidonvilles), which aimed to eradicate slums in urban centers within seven years (2004–10). As a result of this program, more than 167,000 households benefited from improved housing conditions or were rehoused (UN Habitat 2011). Simultaneously, over the 2000–15 period, living standards were improved in 230 cities and urban centers through urban-upgrading programs (programmes de mise à niveau urbaine).[1] In addition, the National Human Development Initiative, whose objectives include combatting social exclusion in urban areas and improving living standards and quality of life of the population, has benefited more than 1.6 million households.

Despite all of their assets, Moroccan cities are not fully delivering on their potential. In addition to accounting for an increasing share of national GDP, cities also generate positive spillovers both for their surrounding metropolitan areas (especially rural areas) and for the country at-large: 80 percent of total tax receipts and 60 percent of total employment stem from urban areas. However, urbanization in Morocco has not generated the same growth benefits as in many other countries with similar contexts. Compared with other countries, Morocco's urbanization occurs at consistently lower levels of GDP per capita, with a slower structural transformation of the economy (transition from primary to secondary and tertiary activities) and a lower share of tradable sectors in the economies of both large and medium cities. These patterns suggest that Morocco needs specific policies to improve returns from its urbanization process.

Countries that have succeeded in leveraging urbanization to spur growth while reducing territorial disparities and differentials in living standards have articulated differentiated and integrated policies to address their specific territorial development challenges. Specific challenges and the policies to address them vary among countries and regions. However, reaping the benefits of both economic concentration and social convergence requires implementing policy actions aimed at economic integration. Integration begins with institutions that ensure access to basic services such as primary education, primary health care, adequate sanitation, and clean drinking water for everyone. As economic integration becomes more difficult, adaptive policies should include roads, railways, airports, harbors, and communication systems that facilitate the movement of goods, services, people, and ideas locally, but also nationally and internationally. For territories where integration is hardest, for social or administrative reasons, the response should include integrated policies, with institutions that unite, infrastructure that connects, and interventions that target, such as slum-upgrading programs or programs focused on specific vulnerable groups.

MOROCCO'S SPECIFIC CHALLENGES IN PROMOTING ECONOMIC INTEGRATION AND SOCIAL CONVERGENCE

This note identifies specific challenges that constrain Morocco's ability to leverage urbanization for economic growth and shared prosperity.

First, constraints linked to land administration, urban and territorial planning, and the financing and provision of basic services are limiting the pace and efficiency of Morocco's urbanization process, posing major constraints to the country's spatial and economic development. Access to land is usually a major factor in blocking or delaying public investment projects (housing, industrial zones, and community infrastructures). Low-income households who cannot afford urban land in the formal market settle in informal settlements or surrounding informal districts (*douars*) without adequate access to basic services. Access to industrial land is also a major constraint to the development of new businesses. A recent study found that removing land market distortions could increase total factor productivity 16 percent. Access to land is also a frequent factor in delay in public investment projects. These constraints not only pose short-term challenges but also contribute to shaping the long-term spatial development of Moroccan cities, which are experiencing urban sprawl.

Second, several factors limit the circulation of people, goods, and ideas within cities as well as between cities and regions. High transport costs within cities keep workers from jobs and people from services. This is particularly true given the tendency toward urban sprawl already mentioned. Morocco's last census confirms the concentration of population around—not within—larger cities. Urban growth is absorbed mainly by the cities' peripheries, leading to a significantly larger urban footprint and substantial sprawl. For example, while the population of Greater Casablanca grew 1.6 percent between the two last censuses, the population of the commune of Casablanca (excluding the peripheral cities) rose only 1 percent. The Rabat-Salé-Kenitra agglomeration grew 1.3 percent, while the population of Rabat itself declined 0.8 percent. Similarly, the population of the Marrakesh-Safi region rose 1.4 percent, while the city of Marrakesh grew only 1.1 percent.

Morocco's economic integration is also impeded by the high cost of transporting goods between cities (representing roughly 17 percent of merchandise value, compared with 7 percent in neighboring countries). This high cost is driven in part by the atomization and poor quality of freight service operators. In spite of several connectivity programs, rural connectivity is relatively low and affected by geographic and climate-related hazards, disadvantaging people living in predominantly rural regions. Finally, the circulation of ideas is limited by the insufficient level of information and communication technology connectivity in Morocco. Fixed broadband penetration as a percentage of households and mobile broadband penetration as a percentage of the population in Morocco are each less than half the average of Middle East and North African countries.

Third, the persistence of pockets of poverty—both in urban and rural areas—and the rise of youth unemployment call for targeted interventions. An inadequately managed and supported urbanization process exacerbates poverty in disadvantaged urban and periurban neighborhoods as well as in certain rural areas. The long-term solution to these challenges rests with improved access to education and to training on connective infrastructure; it also requires immediate targeted interventions to address specific issues of social exclusion. Specifically, integrating young Moroccans (people ages 15–29 account for about 30 percent of Morocco's population and for 44 percent of the working-age population) into the labor market is one of the major challenges for decision makers. Overall, Morocco has more than 1 million unemployed job seekers, 70 percent of whom are ages 15–29 years; additionally, up to 3.5 million youth in this age group are currently not in education, employment, or training, most of whom live in urban areas.

ADDRESSING MOROCCO'S MAIN CHALLENGES IN THE CONTEXT OF THE GOVERNMENT'S DECENTRALIZATION AGENDA

Morocco has embarked on an ambitious institutional reform agenda aimed at deepening decentralization (through Advanced Regionalization laws) and deconcentration (through the Deconcentration Charter). The ongoing institutional reforms introduced through the 2011 Constitution represent a unique opportunity for Morocco to proceed in a more relevant and effective way by aligning mandates, resources, and capacities at different scales—national, regional, and local (see box ES.1).

Empowering municipalities, both financially and institutionally, is key to addressing the constraints identified for access to land and basic services. The decentralization reforms confirmed the central role of municipalities in the provision of key basic services that are critical to efficient urbanization. Although the reforms gave them more autonomy, municipalities still face mounting challenges to step up to the task of delivering the infrastructure needed to accommodate the continued increase in urban population. Indeed, it is estimated that Morocco's urban municipalities will need to multiply their current investment level by five in order to accommodate future investment needs.

This large expansion of investment is possible, provided that all available levers are used to improve the framework for municipal finance. These levers include (a) increasing the predictability of and improving the current mechanisms for fiscal transfers, (b) improving the return on taxes administered by the central government on behalf of the municipalities and on taxes administered directly by municipalities, (c) simplifying and reforming Law 47-06 relative to local taxation to achieve higher returns, and (d) leveraging increased net savings

Box ES.1

Territorial organization: A three-level political-administrative system

The Moroccan territory is divided into 12 regions, 75 provinces (including 13 urban prefectures and 62 rural provinces), and 1,538 municipalities. These three territorial levels are administered by decentralized authorities: municipal councils, provincial councils, and, since the 2011 constitutional reform, regional councils whose members are elected by universal suffrage. The state's deconcentrated organization is based mainly on this territorial division: the *wali* is the highest representative of the central authority at this deconcentrated level and exercises jurisdiction at a regional level (within the *wilaya*), while the governor exercises jurisdiction at the prefecture and provincial level.

In 1976 Morocco initiated a decentralization process through the first municipal charter. Morocco stands out from other Middle East and North African countries by according a high level of financing to local administrations—3.5 percent of gross national product, compared with only 1 percent in Tunisia, for instance—and by devolving important functions to them (including, for example, roadways, public areas, urban transport, waste, water, sanitation, and hygiene). The 2011 Constitution and related organic laws allocate important financial resources to the 12 regions and expand their competencies in the areas of economic development, vocational training, land planning, public transportation, and protection of the environment.

and creditworthiness through increased and sustainable borrowing. Beyond their financial capacity, municipalities also need to ramp up their capacity to plan for and execute investments over the short, middle, and long term, based on their assigned objectives for development and access to basic services. Improving capacity is the purpose of the Municipal Development Plans (Plans d'action communaux [PACs]), a new generation of documents introduced by the government for technical and budget planning. Their implementation should be supported with all means available to improve municipal governance and technical capabilities.

The legal framework for intermunicipal cooperation needs to be strengthened to support the management of cities at the right scale. Urbanization in Morocco is leading to metropolization, with larger cities growing beyond municipal boundaries. The introduction of intermunicipal cooperation establishments (etablissements de cooperation intercommunale [ECIs]) in Organic Law 113-14 on municipalities was intended to provide metropolitan agglomerations with a framework for service delivery at the intermunicipal level. Morocco has already launched several ECIs (Al Assima for the Greater Rabat and Al Baida for the Greater Casablanca) on a voluntary basis. However, the legal and institutional framework for intermunicipal cooperation will require further development. The note outlines priorities, including (a) providing ECIs with a framework for financial sustainability and autonomy, (b) extending their responsibilities to the delivery of major urban public services, and (c) ensuring their emergence at a relevant geographic scale.

Municipalities or their ECIs should take a greater role in urban and territorial planning. Diffused and uncoordinated responsibilities for territorial planning and infrastructure provision contribute to the constraints related to access to land and fragmented urban expansion. Building on the ongoing decentralization reforms,[2] Morocco can strengthen the pivotal role of local governments in planning for and financing urban development. Urban agencies, a key component of the Moroccan system, should focus their efforts on supporting and building the capacity of local administrations to take a larger role in urban and territorial planning, in compliance with Article 85 of Organic Law 113-14, which requires the execution of the provisions of the Land Use Plan (Plan d'aménagement [PA]) and the Rural Development Plan (Plan de développement des agglomérations rurales [PDAR]). Local governments should be empowered to raise revenues from the new developments taking place in their territory through rationalized development taxes and improved data on land and property values. Finally, local governments could use the institutional structure of joint-ownership companies (sociétés de développement local [SDLs]) to promote strategic urban operations in their territory in partnership with the private sector.

Improving connectivity within cities will require coordinated action from local and national governments. Improving the circulation of people within cities requires coordinated action between multiple actors to improve the efficiency, sustainability, and affordability of urban transport. Local governments or their ECIs have a central role to play in improving the efficiency of urban transport (especially public transport) and mobility by integrating this key component more closely with urban planning (Urban Development Master Plan—Schéma directeur d'aménagement urbain [SDAU]—and PA). Local governments, together with the national government, also have a determining role to play in ensuring the financial sustainability and affordability of urban transport services. They can play this role by providing adequate and sustainable financial resources for the operation of urban transport services and the development of well-targeted subsidies, as well as the implementation of necessary regulatory measures.

Regional councils will have a key role to play in ensuring the adequate coordination and articulation of sectoral policies for their territories. The Advanced Regionalization reforms have significantly expanded the region's own competencies to boost development and the social and economic integration of populations. As a tier of government in charge of economic development, vocational training, and employment, regional councils should be at the forefront of the formulation and implementation of targeted interventions aimed at improving opportunities for specific vulnerable groups such as unemployed youths. Regions also have a central role to play in the development of connective infrastructure, through the identification and development of regional and interregional transport corridors.

The central government should continue playing a supporting role and should implement key reforms to clarify the rules of the game, empower local governments, deconcentrate its decision-making power, and provide public and private actors with the right incentives. The national government should pursue long-term reforms in order to improve its ability to manage lands and property rights, control and regulate spatial development, strengthen institutions for land management and service provision, and improve urban transport infrastructure and financing. The government would also benefit from improved regulation of the freight industry to reduce its atomization, incentivize formality and renewal of fleets, invest in select interregional corridors, and facilitate greater digital connectivity and broadband penetration. Finally, public authorities have an important role to play in ensuring the availability of adequate spatial, economic, and social data in order for local administrations to design and target their programs and assessments.

NOTES

1. See Kingdom of Morocco, Ministry of the Interior, Territorial Collectivities national portal: http://www.pncl.gov.ma.
2. Including Article 85 of Organic Law 113-14, which mandates that municipalities be responsible for "the execution of the provisions of the PA [Land Use Plan] and PDAR [Rural Development Plan]" ("l'exécution des dispositions du PA et du PDAR") and "the opening of new urbanization areas in accordance with the procedures and conditions determined by regulation" ("l'ouverture de nouvelles zones à l'urbanisation conformément à des modalités et des conditions fixées par voie réglementaire").

REFERENCES

HCP (Haut Commissariat au Plan). 2013. "National Employment Survey." Rabat: HCP.

King Mohammed VI. 2017. "Un nouveau modèle de développement à même de répondre aux aspirations de toutes les catégories de la population et d'être en phase avec les évolutions que connaît le pays." King's speech at opening of parliament, October 13.

UN Habitat. 2011. "Evaluation du programme national 'Villes sans Bidonvilles': Propositions pour en accroitre les performances." UN Habitat, Nairobi.

Abbreviations

ECI	intermunicipal cooperation establishment/établissement de cooperation intercommunale
GDP	gross domestic product
GVA	gross value added
IT	information technology
LGRCIS	Local Government Revenue Collection Information System
OECD	Organisation for Economic Co-operation and Development
PA	Land Use Plan/Plan d'aménagement
PAC	Municipal Development Plan/Plan d'action communal
PDAR	Rural Development Plan/Plan de développement des agglomérations rurales
PDU	Urban Mobility Plan/Plan de déplacement urbain
PSP	private sector participation
SAR	special administrative region
SDAU	Urban Development Master Plan/Schéma directeur d'aménagement urbain
SDL	joint-ownership company/société de développement local
TFP	total factor productivity
WDR	World Development Report

1. Introduction: Well-Managed Urbanization Is Central to Morocco's Development

Getting urbanization right is a key challenge for Morocco's development. Urbanization and the rising population density and production in cities are two of the most striking features of economic development. Incomes tend to rise with urban density, especially when accompanied by increases in the contribution of industry and services to economic activity and jobs. In Morocco, getting urbanization right is central because it would address three pressing needs:

- *Economic need* to diversify the national economy away from the primary sector—half of Morocco's labor force is engaged in agriculture despite urbanization rates higher than 50 percent.
- *Social need* to reduce spatial disparities in living standards between rural and urban areas—living standards measured by per capita household consumption are 54 percent lower in rural areas than in urban areas.
- *Political need* to create jobs for more than 1 million unemployed job seekers, most of whom are between the ages of 15 and 29.

Well-managed cities are critical for Morocco's transformation into upper-middle income and beyond. Evidence from today's high-income and rapidly emerging economies shows that urbanization is a source of dynamism that can lead to enhanced productivity. No country in the industrial age has ever achieved significant economic growth without urbanization. When managed well, urbanization leads the structural shift from agriculture to manufacturing and service activities. At the same time, income per capita tends to rise as the share of the urban population increases.

Urbanization is rapidly unfolding in Morocco, with increasing concentration of people and economic activity in urban areas. Economic activity is concentrated around the largest cities, alongside spikes of activity in smaller towns and urban areas. These patterns of economic concentration are consistent with global experience. Only 1.5 percent of the world's land is home to half of its production. In France and Japan, both high-income countries, Paris and Tokyo concentrate more than 30 percent and 40 percent of their nation's economic activity in less than 2 percent and 4 percent of the country's land, respectively (Kochendorfer-Lucius and Pleskovic 2009). The underlying mechanism fueling the benefits of economic density are "agglomeration economies," which enhance productivity via three key mechanisms: (a) lowering transport costs, (b) developing markets for specialized services, and (c) matching labor markets (see box 1.1 for details).

Productivity gains are closely linked with the urbanization process, which goes hand in hand with structural transformations and industrialization. As countries urbanize, workers move from rural to urban areas in search of better-paying and more productive jobs. Similarly, entrepreneurs locate their firms in cities where agglomeration economies will increase their productivity. Close spatial proximity has many benefits. Certain public goods—like infrastructure and basic services—are cheaper to provide when populations are large and densely concentrated. Firms located near each other can share suppliers, lowering input costs. Thick labor markets reduce search costs, enabling firms to choose from a larger pool of workers whenever they need to hire additional labor. And spatial proximity makes it easier for workers to share information and learn from one another. International examples show that knowledge spillovers play a key role in boosting the productivity of successful cities.

However, many policy makers in Morocco are worried about rising economic concentration in cities. They are concerned that urbanization is exacerbating spatial inequalities and often consider options to divert economic and population growth to underserved periurban areas. The evidence suggests that these worries are unfounded and that policy efforts need to be redirected. Rather than worry about the size of cities such as Casablanca and Rabat, policy makers should examine whether Moroccan cities are generating agglomeration economies, which enhance trade linkages among each other as well as across the Mediterranean and beyond (box 1.2). Figure 1.1 clearly shows that the peaks of economic activity in Northern Africa, particularly in Morocco, are actually small in the broader economic landscape. For Morocco to cross the threshold into upper-middle income and beyond, economic concentration will need to rise. At the same time, complementary policies are needed to ensure that the benefits of economic concentration are shared with all residents—in rural and urban areas alike.

BOX 1.1

Urban pattern in Morocco: A city system organized along the Atlantic urban axis

The Moroccan city system is dominated by its economic capital, Casablanca, and is characterized by substantial urbanization of the Casablanca-Mohammedia-Rabat-Salé-Kenitra Atlantic axis, accounting for more than 40 percent of the country's total urban population in 2016. Over the last decades, six metropolises of greater than 100,000 inhabitants have developed, including Marrakesh (in the foothills of the Atlas Mountains) and Agadir (on the Atlantic coast), whose economies are based mainly on tourism, and most recently Tangier in northern Morocco, which is the second largest national economic center and has been influenced by the development of Tangier Med, a cruise and cargo port. Small cities have been growing even faster than larger agglomerations (the demographic weight of those large agglomerations on total urban population tends to decrease proportionally).

Given the potential economic benefits of cities, it is not surprising that urbanization and economic development go hand in hand. The evidence from China, the Republic of Korea, and Vietnam highlights the close association between episodes of rapid urbanization and economic development. These links are evident in Morocco, but they could be stronger, with urbanization leading economic progress, not simply following it. In fact, cities have historically been located in places with inherent natural advantages, such as coastal locations with proximity to ports or fertile agricultural land. This is not surprising, given that natural endowments such as the fertility of land (suitable for agriculture), temperature, precipitation, and proximity to the coast explain 56 percent of the variation in economic performance across Morocco's territory, with agroclimatic conditions being more important correlates of prosperity than in neighboring Algeria and Tunisia.[1]

BOX 1.2

Agglomeration economies

By generating "agglomeration economies," cities can be instrumental in enhancing productivity and spurring innovation and economic diversification. The underlying reason for this process is density. The most basic agglomeration economy is the reduction of transport costs for goods. If a supplier locates near customers, the costs of shipping decline. In the early 1900s, London and New York were manufacturing powerhouses, places where factories located to be close to customers and transport infrastructure. And in the late 19th century, four-fifths of Chicago's jobs were compactly located within four miles of State and Maddison streets, close to where people lived and infrastructure was available (Goswami and Lall 2015). Many of these benefits increase with larger scale; towns and small cities cannot reap the same benefits as larger cities do. International evidence suggests that the elasticity of income per capita with respect to urban population is between 3 percent and 8 percent (Rosenthal and Strange 2003). Each doubling of a city's size raises its productivity 5 percent.

The density and size of cities can also create a market for specialized services, including legal support, advertising, logistics, and management consulting. These services are critical for young firms, enabling them to focus on their big idea and core competence without having to worry about supporting functions. The larger the cluster, the more specialized the service providers can be. Think of New York City, where a young fashion designer does not need an in-house lawyer to manage intellectual property and incorporation; she can use a logistics firm to connect with merchandisers in Hong Kong SAR, China, or production houses outside of Colombo, Sri Lanka.

In addition, cities are also instrumental in matching skills with job opportunities, and density allows for an integrated "thick" labor market. In fact, skills matching will gain much more importance over the next 20 years as the current generation of Moroccan children gets better educated than their parents and searches more intensively for jobs that fully reward their skills. Just as many Indian children who grew up to become software engineers in the 1990s lined up to move to Bangalore, where many software firms are concentrated, getting cities such as Casablanca and Tangier to flourish can help Moroccan children to find jobs with companies that specifically target their profile and are willing to pay for their skill set. Research in the United States shows that workers living in cities where the number of college graduates is increasing experience more rapid salary gains than workers living in cities where the number of college graduates is stagnating (Moretti 2004). This relationship is particularly strong for workers with high-tech jobs. Well-functioning cities that nurture and attract skills and enable density-based interactions can help the current generation of Moroccan children to harness the urban advantage (map B1.2.1).

continued

BOX 1.2, *continued*

MAP B1.2.1

Mountains of economic activity in Morocco and Northern Africa

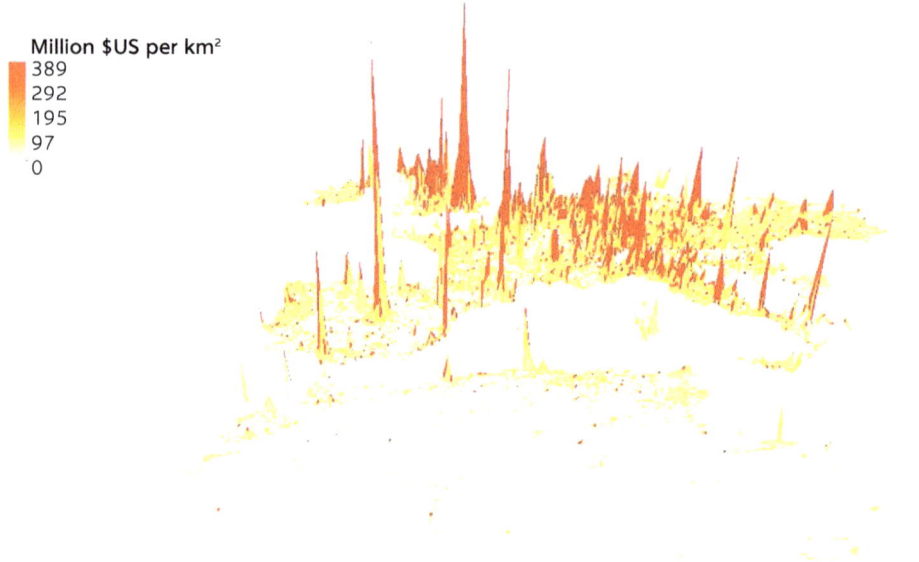

Source: Ghosh et al. 2010.

URBANIZATION AND THE DELIVERY OF ECONOMIC AND SOCIAL DIVIDENDS

However, urbanization has not generated the same growth benefits in Morocco as it has in many other countries. In 1960, Morocco's urbanization rate was close to 30 percent, while its gross domestic product (GDP) per capita was less than US$600 (constant 2005 U.S. dollars). Only 11 countries had lower GDP per capita than Morocco when they crossed the 30 percent urbanization mark. The same pattern can be seen when Morocco crossed the 50 percent urbanization mark in 1993 (figure 1.1). Many of the countries that have achieved greater economic performance for the same urbanization level have GDP per capita at least twice that of Morocco. These patterns suggest that specific policies are needed for Morocco to derive higher returns from its urbanization process.

Moreover, urbanization in Morocco has not been accompanied by structural transformation and thus has not created enough jobs (figure 1.2). Although more than 50 percent urban, Morocco still employs about half of its labor

Introduction: Well-Managed Urbanization Is Central to Morocco's Development | 5

FIGURE 1.1
GDP per capita in countries at 50% urbanization level

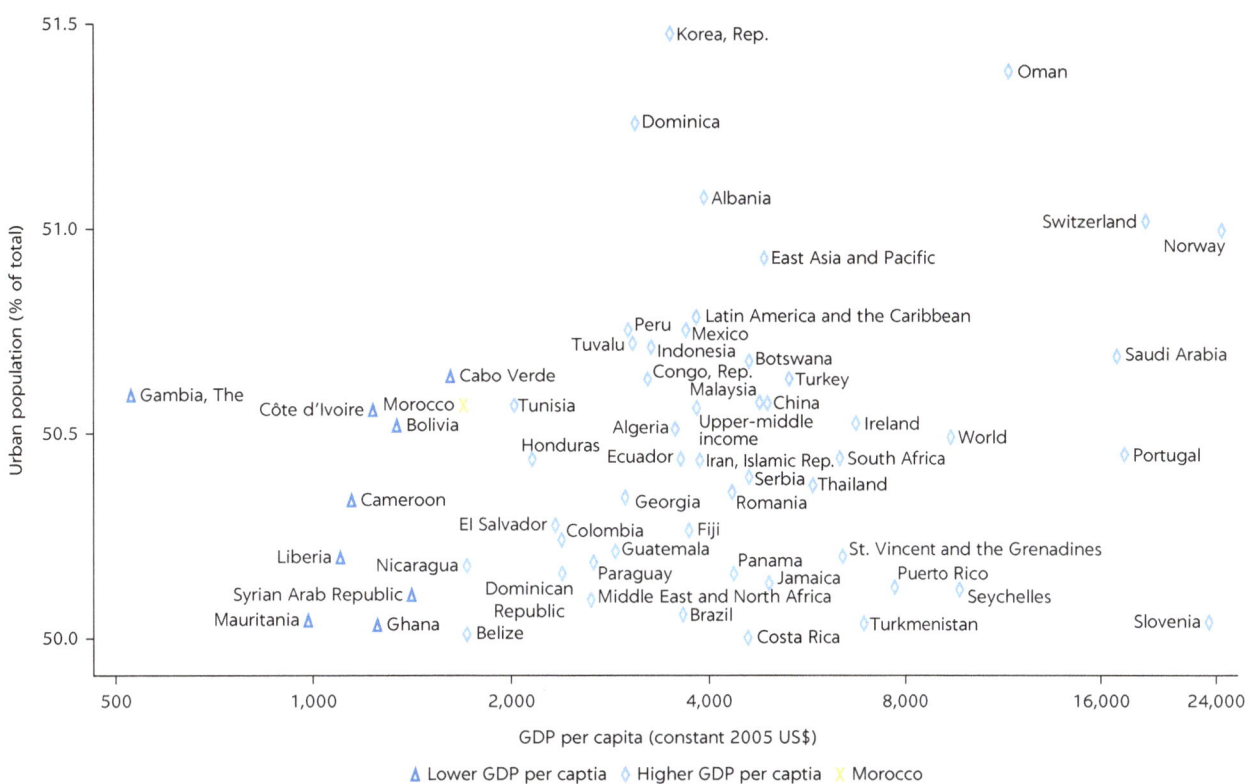

Source: Analysis based on Oxford Economics data for 2015.

FIGURE 1.2
Urbanization rate in Morocco, 2000–14

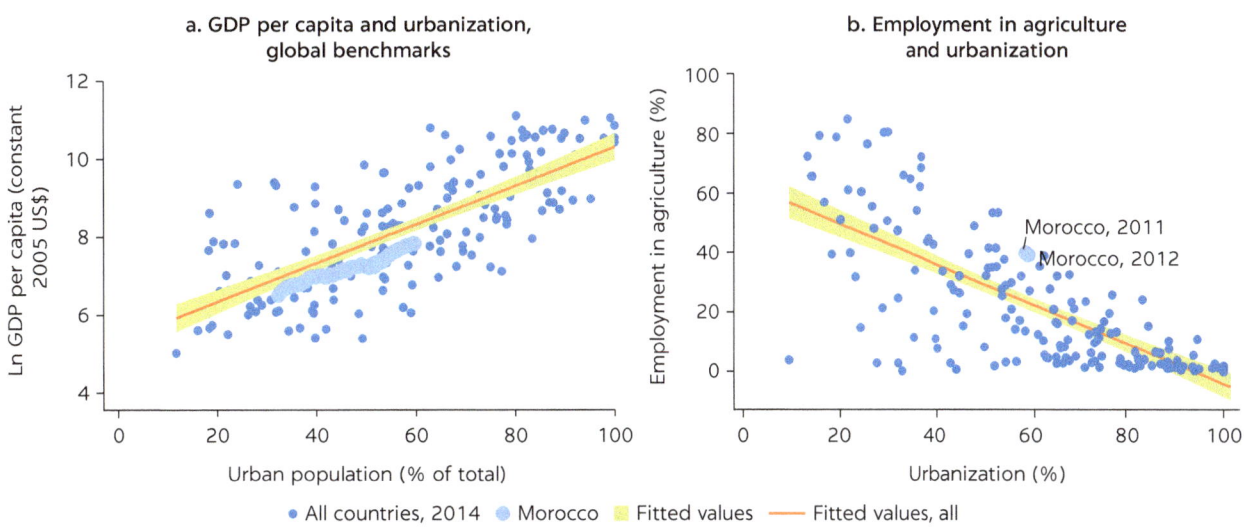

Source: World Bank calculations based on World Development Indicators.
Note: Panel b uses the latest employment data available in the period 2000–14.

force in agriculture. The movement of urban workers into manufacturing and high-value services has been minimal, affecting productivity and the creation of more complex and diversified economic structures.

There is a clear difference in the stage of the economic structure between primary agglomerations (Casablanca and Rabat) and secondary agglomerations (Agadir, Fes, Marrakesh, Meknes, and Tangier), which appear to be lagging behind the country's structural transformation. Figure 1.3 shows the sectoral share of employment and gross value added across three broad sectors—agriculture, manufacturing, and services[2]—in 775 cities across the globe, including the 7 largest Moroccan agglomerations and 10 comparator cities[3] from different regions and at different levels of GDP per capita. Morocco's primary agglomerations—especially Casablanca—have the highest share of employees working in high-value services, with a rate above the world average. In contrast, Morocco's secondary cities employ a far lower percentage of workers in high-value services, while keeping a significantly high rate of employment in the agriculture sector (14.5 percent). Further efforts to enable secondary cities to become economies with higher-productivity sectors are necessary to propel economic growth and reduce regional disparities. These processes require, among others, high levels of human capital and skilled workers trained in the use of new technologies, active support and promotion of private sector investments, and flexible labor markets. If young migrants find no opportunities for education and better-paying jobs, labor could easily migrate to less productive sectors, thus jeopardizing structural change.

Firms in Moroccan cities are producing mostly locally consumed or nontradable goods and services (figure 1.4), which compounds the challenges of structural transformation. This situation is challenging for developing the urban economy, as the consumer base of one city, however large, is much smaller than that of a regional or global market. Specializing in nontradables for local consumption leads to diminishing returns (for both technological and price reasons). In contrast, export markets are key to a dynamic industrial sector. Structural weaknesses translate into lower economic growth, with major Moroccan cities growing slower—4.8 percent—than their peers (figure 1.5). The drivers of the preponderant share of nontradable goods and services in the economies of Moroccan cities are likely related to macro and micro dynamics that deserve further investigation.

Despite a decade of sustained economic growth, Moroccan cities are still lagging behind in key areas for competitiveness. As shown in figures 1.6 and 1.7, set against comparator cities from different regions and levels of income, Moroccan cities display low levels of labor productivity and low rates of formal employment as a share of the working-age population.

While cities are not fully leveraging their economic potential, spatial disparities in living standards between rural and urban areas remain large and persistent. Household consumption per capita is 54 percent lower in rural areas than in urban areas. And access to services compounds welfare differentials, with access rates varying significantly across regions by type of area (urban or rural) across a range of basic services. For example, there is one doctor for 935 residents in Greater Casablanca—the most urbanized region, which is 3.5 times more than in Taza, the least urbanized region. This issue is elaborated further in chapter 2.

Taken together, the combination of low returns in cities and large rural-urban disparities is a major source of concern for Morocco's policy makers. Moroccan cities have an opportunity to overcome these challenges and be at the forefront

FIGURE 1.3
Sectoral shares of employment and value added in the 7 largest Moroccan agglomerations, 10 comparator cities, and 775 cities vs. GDP per capita, 2015

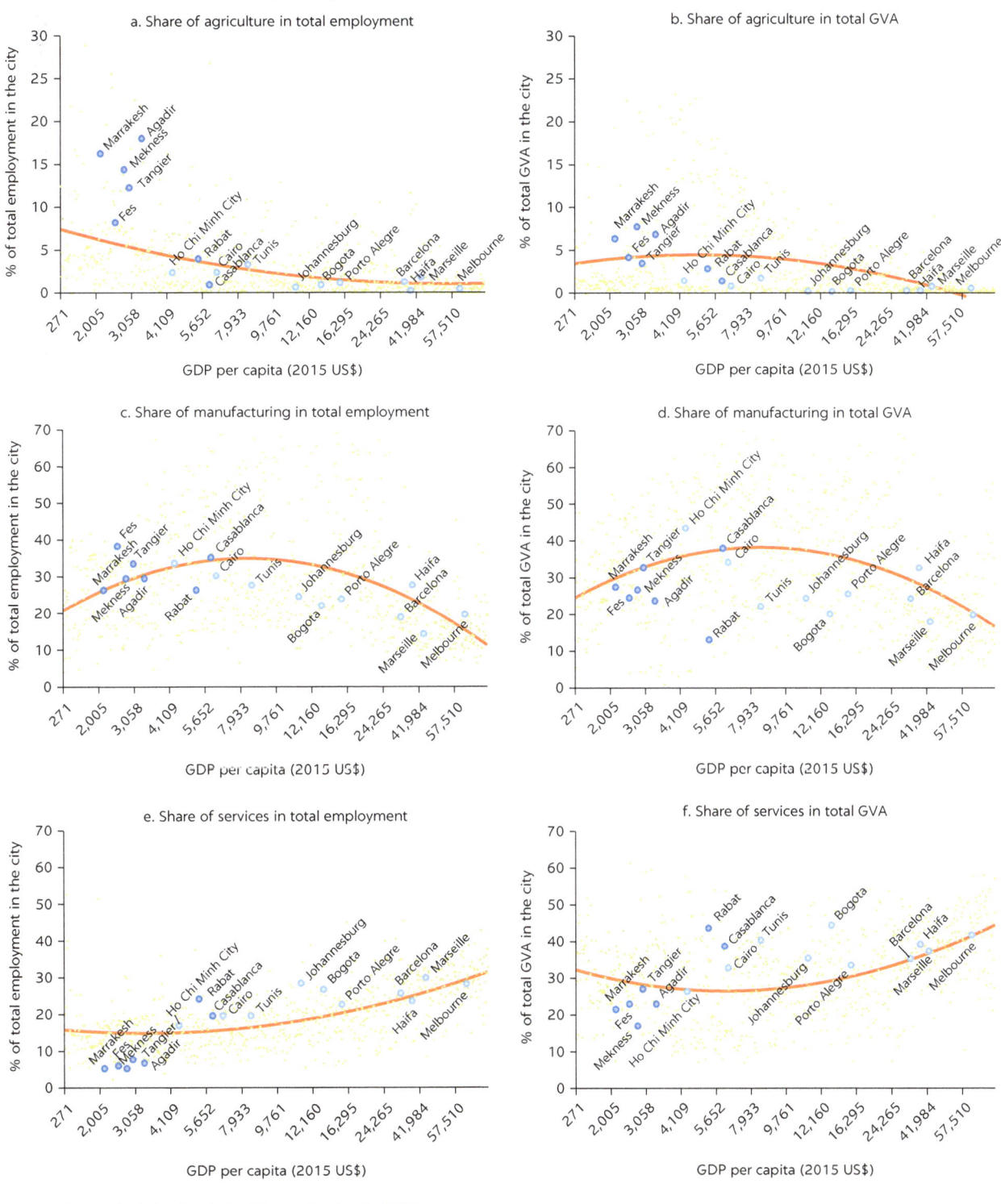

Source: Analysis using Oxford Economics data for 2015.
Note: GVA = gross value added.

FIGURE 1.4

Share of firms in internationally traded and nontradable sectors in select cities in low- and middle-income countries (latest post-2010 data)

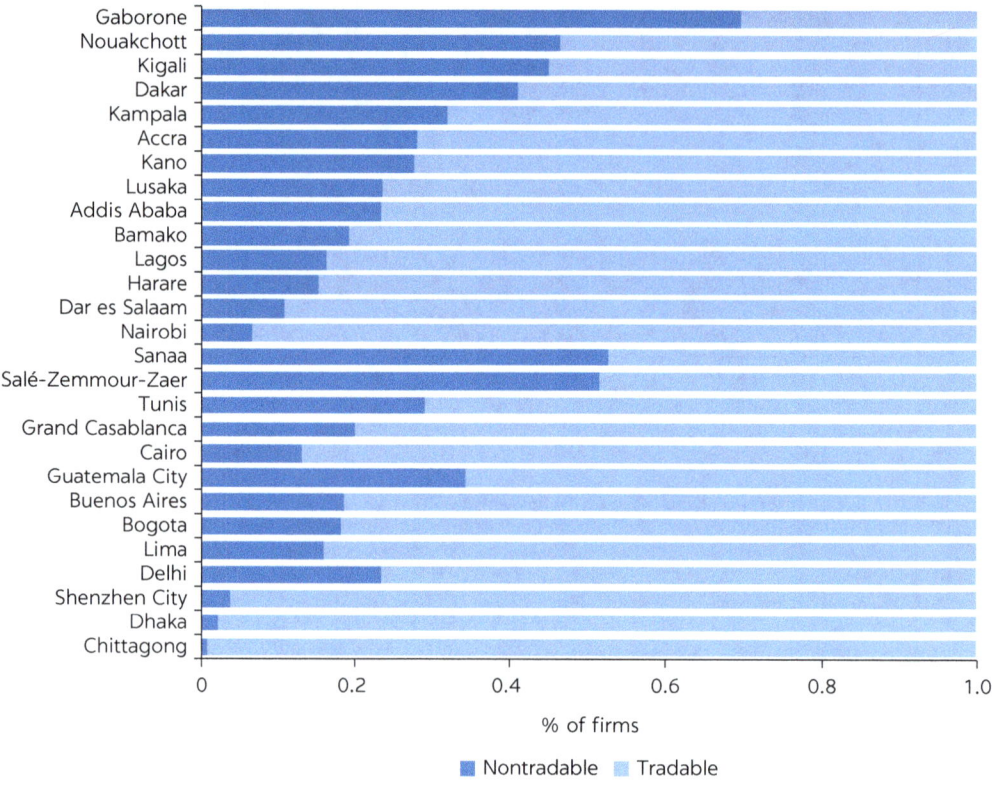

Source: Calculation based on the World Bank Enterprise Surveys.

FIGURE 1.5

Economic growth of Moroccan cities compared with global comparators, 2005–15

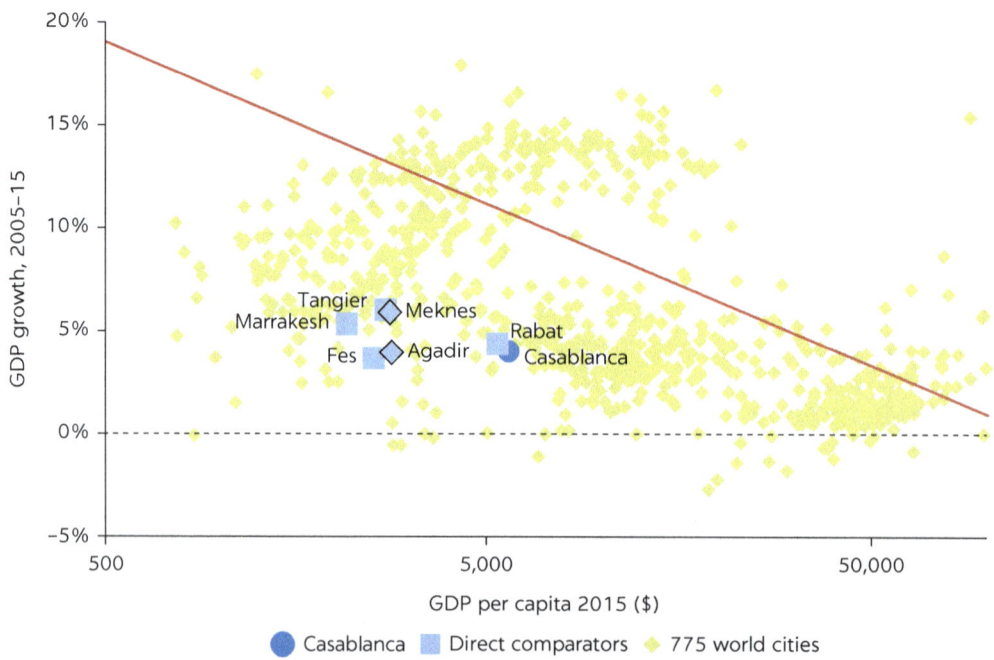

Source: Analysis using Oxford Economics data for 2015.

FIGURE 1.6
Labor productivity in cities in Morocco and in select countries, 2015

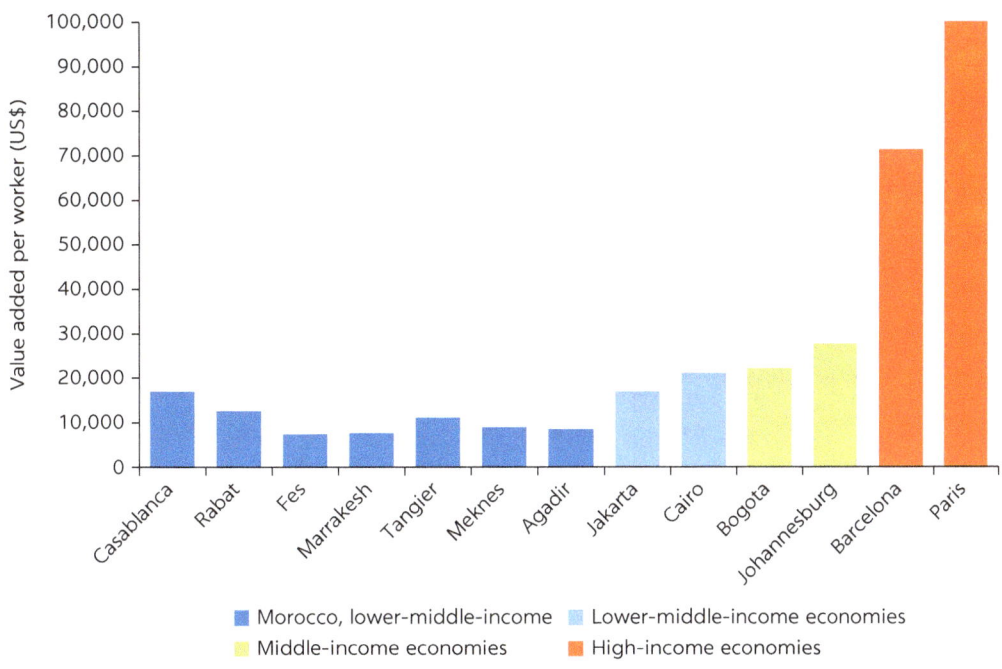

Source: Analysis using Oxford Economics data for 2015.

FIGURE 1.7
Employment as a share of working-age population in cities in Morocco and in select countries, 2015

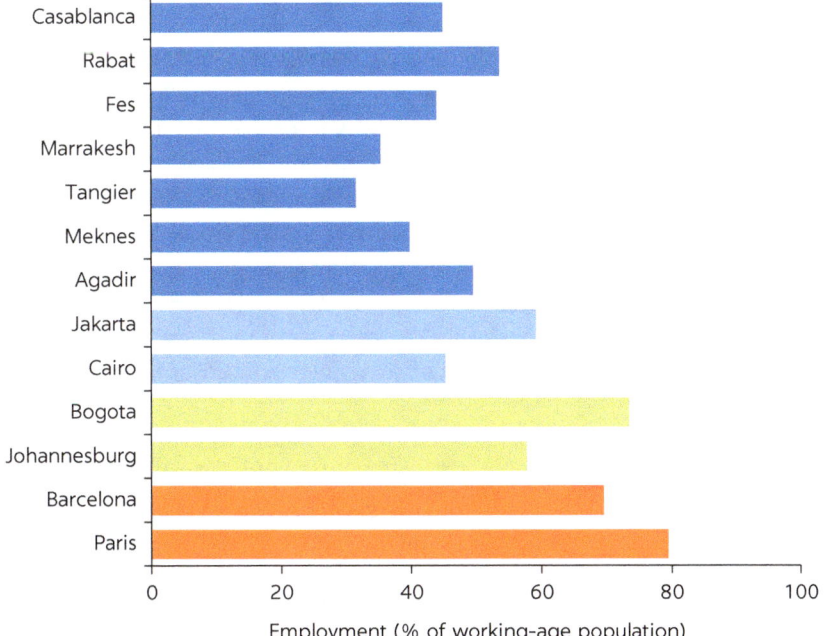

Source: Analysis using Oxford Economics data for 2015.

in contributing to rapid job creation and economic growth as well as social and spatial inclusion. Cities offer proximity and scale that can lower the costs of infrastructure, utilities, and service provision. They also can contribute to increasing employment opportunities provided that firms are concentrated in a single area, making economies of scale possible. Firms benefit from being close to their suppliers and to consumers of their products; they also benefit from proximity to other firms with which they can share technologies and information. Yet, inequalities in living standards can adversely affect national unity, weaken social cohesion, and foster political instability. Global experience shows that persistent spatial disparities in living standards are neither desirable nor inevitable.

HOW CAN MOROCCO'S LEADERS MAKE URBANIZATION WORK BETTER FOR SHARED PROSPERITY?

Morocco undertook significant efforts to support urban development, showing its willingness to take a sustainable approach to developing cities. Morocco has important legislative and regulatory resources to support urban development, as illustrated by the first decree (*dahir*) on urban planning in 1914. Since that time, its urban expertise has developed significantly, which has led to a new format of urban documents aiming to strengthen urban-rural complementarity. The adoption of major related international agreements (Sustainable Development Goals, New Urban Agenda, Sendai Framework, and the Council of Parties 22), several sectoral strategies in urban management (Sustainable Development National Strategy and the Energy Efficiency National Strategy), and several ongoing discussions (including the National Land Management Strategy and the territorial dialogue conducted with different partners) illustrate Morocco's high commitment to sustainable urban development.

With regard to public policy options, differentiated policies tailored to specific urbanization challenges met by Morocco at multiple levels are likely to be the most effective. This graduated set of policy priorities should recognize that the problems get harder as urbanization proceeds. In places that are mostly rural, the aim is to implement "neutral" policies toward rural and urban areas and to set in place the foundations for a good urbanization process. This approach requires taking care of the basics in towns and villages and promoting functioning land markets, school systems, sanitation, and security. Local governments cannot undertake these actions easily—they are mainly the responsibility of central states, as the good track record of governments in Costa Rica and Korea shows.

Additionally, local governments have to do more to keep urbanization inclusive in places that are urbanizing rapidly. Although urbanization has been strongly associated with poverty reduction, the "stubborn realities" of inequalities in cities have persisted (McGranahan, Schensul, and Singh 2016). Lack of opportunities and lack of access to quality urban services are at the root of inequalities. Inequalities also come with spatial segregation, which is quite costly to reverse. It is therefore crucial for local governments to eliminate discriminatory exclusion, create more equitable markets, services, and public spaces, and guarantee human rights within the urban space. This effort requires effective regulation of land markets, urban planning, and implementation of infrastructure and institutions for improved access to public services for the benefit of all, including poor and marginalized populations.

In places with high urbanization rates, above 75 percent in Casablanca, even more difficulties must be considered. In such places, the top concern becomes living conditions or livability. Livability requires good land administration, good schools, and good transport as well as programs to integrate slums into the broader urban landscape. This effort requires coordination between local governments and authorities. Cities like Hong Kong SAR, China, and Singapore could do this more easily because city, state, and central governments are essentially the same. But cities such as Bogotá, Seoul, and Shanghai show that this can be done even in bigger countries such as China, Colombia, and Korea.

What do these principles imply for Morocco? Policy makers would benefit from treating cities, towns, and rural areas as a portfolio of assets, each differentiated by characteristics that include the size, location, and density of settlement.

- *In towns located in predominantly rural regions, such as Taza,* the priority should be to set in place common institutions related to the regulation of land markets and the provision of basic social services like schools, sanitation, and security. Institution building aims to ensure a level playing field for people and entrepreneurs throughout the country. Institution-building policies should therefore not take into account the spatial dimension (that is, not distinguish within or across the rural or urban space).
- *In cities that are urbanizing rapidly, such as Meknes and Tangier,* besides putting in place the institutions governing land markets and providing social services, the priority is to invest in connective infrastructure so that the benefits of economic density are shared more widely with the cities' hinterlands, and Morocco's coastal cities can leverage their natural comparative advantage as global trade nodes: places such as Tangier are well suited to be interlocutors between Morocco and global markets, particularly those across the Mediterranean Sea.
- *In major cities where rapid urbanization has long been a reality, such as Casablanca and Rabat,* the priority should be to foster city competitiveness for more and better jobs and to address social inclusion through targeted interventions, such as improved mobility for vulnerable and poor populations, urban youth employment programs, and slum-upgrading programs. However, without effective institutions, targeted social and spatial inclusion interventions, and connective infrastructures, these interventions are unlikely to work.

The next chapter of this note examines specific policy areas where reforms can help to harness the external benefits of urbanization in Morocco.

NOTES

1. Based on econometric analysis conducted for this report using luminosity and natural endowments.
2. Services include high-end business services, transport, and information and communication technology.
3. The selected cities vary from low-middle-income to high-income economies across all regions in the world; most of them are in countries with decentralized political and economic systems.

REFERENCES

Ghosh, T., R. L. Powell, C. D. Elvidge, K. E. Baugh, P. C. Sutton, and S. Anderson. 2010. "Shedding Light on the Global Distribution of Economic Activity." *Open Geography Journal* 3 (1): 148–61.

Goswami, Arti Grover, and Somic V. Lall. 2015. "Spatial Dispersion of Jobs in an African City: Evidence from Kampala." World Bank, Washington, DC. http://conference.iza.org/conference_files/worldb2015/grover%20goswami_a22129.pdf.

Kochendorfer-Lucius, Gudrun, and Boris Pleskovic, eds. 2009. *Spatial Disparities and Development Policy*. Berlin Workshop Series 2009. Washington, DC: World Bank.

McGranahan, Gordon, Daniel Schensul, and Gayatri Singh. 2016. "Inclusive Urbanization: Can the 2030 Agenda Be Delivered without It?" *Environment and Urbanization* 28 (1): 13–34.

Moretti, Enrico. 2004. "Estimating the Social Return to Higher Education: Evidence from Longitudinal and Repeated Cross-Sectional Data." *Journal of Econometrics* 121 (2004) 175–212.

Rosenthal, Stuart S., and William C. Strange. 2003. "Evidence on the Nature and Sources of Agglomeration Economies." In *Handbook of Regional and Urban Economics*, ch. 49, edited by J. Vernon Henderson, Jacques-François Thisse, 2119–71. Amsterdam: Elsevier.

2 Identifying Key Opportunities for Policy and Investment: Institutions, Infrastructure, and Interventions

Morocco can tackle its urban challenges through a mix of policies focusing on institutions, infrastructure, and interventions:

- *Institutions for land, decentralized service provision, and finance.* At the heart of slow job creation in cities is a poor business environment. Such an environment stems in part from institutional deficiencies that relate to urban land management and uncoordinated institutional responsibilities for urban planning, rules for basic service provision, and inadequate systems of urban finance. As such, the following actions are recommended:

    a. Clarifying land rights and management systems, which will allow cities to plan better and tax for sustainable expansion
    b. Reforming the rules for basic service provision, which will enable services to reach the urban poor, helping to improve standards of living and reduce poverty
    c. Improving systems of urban finance, which will help local governments to improve their capacity to plan for and execute investments that fall under their direct responsibility, thus increasing local accountability and limiting central government's exposure to the widening urban infrastructure gap

- *Infrastructure (spatial connectivity).* More investment is needed in connective infrastructure and services. High transport costs within cities keep workers from accessing jobs and people from accessing services. Lack of investments in connectivity leads to high labor market fragmentation, further reducing mobility and preventing clustering and attendant agglomeration effects. Investment in interregional corridors and mass urban transit will improve connectivity, boost productivity, and help to reduce regional disparities.
- *Interventions (spatial targeting).* Institutional reforms and increased investments in infrastructure will go a long way toward generating a national urban system that is conducive to job-creating enterprises and poverty reduction. But additional targeted interventions will be necessary, especially in the largest metropolitan areas, to address the large and growing challenge of youth unemployment, social exclusion, and limited female labor force participation.

The exceptionally high rates of youth unemployment and exclusion relative to comparator countries are a cause for concern for Moroccan decision makers, and the interventions needed to achieve better outcomes vary by location.

INSTITUTIONS FOR LAND MANAGEMENT, DECENTRALIZED SERVICE PROVISION, AND URBAN FINANCE: WHAT'S NEXT?

Challenge 1: Clarifying land rights and management systems to facilitate investment and help cities to plan

Morocco needs a clearer legal framework and stronger institutions for land management. The country inherited from the protectorate a regulatory and normative approach to urban development, with complex land laws and multiple legal land statuses, which have hindered the development of equipped land and resulted in fragmented urban spaces. The modern system of land registration (immatriculation), which is administered by the Land Conservation, Cartography, and Cadaster National Agency (Agence Nationale de la Conservation Foncière, du Cadastre et de la Cartographie) provides for land rights clarification and titling, but as of today, while 90 percent of land is registered (immatriculé) in urban areas, only 60 percent of land is registered in suburban areas and only 40 percent in rural areas. Besides, land registration is not mandatory. The complexity of land administration seems to be a key bottleneck. The slow pace of official land registration encourages landowners to sell their property according to customary procedures. This situation favors the creation of new informal settlements and encourages developers to begin construction before obtaining their titles, resulting in costly litigation and constraints to infrastructure development. In addition, there is no planning for land acquisition, especially for equipment supply and housing programs.

A fluid land market and faster rollout of land titling would help to improve the business environment (World Bank 2008). Uncertainty over land information and the high costs entailed in discovering the status of land add costs and risks, which slows the pace of land market operations. Transparent systems for ownership, oversight, spatial regulation, and valuation of land parcels in and around cities could help to reduce these costs, improving the ability of poor and middle-income families to access secure holdings and grow their wealth, develop their businesses, and afford proper housing.

At the national level, the Moroccan government should start with improving land governance, simplifying and increasing the pace of land titling, building on the existing immatriculation system, and better linking the land administration system to an overall national strategy for the land sector, as announced by the head of government in 2017 in the aftermath of the national conference on the state land policy.[1] Such reforms are the goals of the National Land Management Strategy and the associated action plan, which will be defined by the government of Morocco with the support of the Millennium Challenge Corporation. At the local level, linking land supply more closely with demand through effective municipal programs would empower local governments and cities to use and integrate land administration tools in order to shape land strategies for housing and equipment supply. These efforts are particularly important in large cities, where providing land for affordable housing construction is a major challenge.

Fragmented urban expansion

Major Moroccan cities are experiencing a process of urban expansion characterized by a decrease of densities in the inner cities, densification of suburban areas, and leapfrogging. Urban sprawl of Morocco's main cities is characterized by leapfrogging, in which scattered developments in the form of housing or tourism projects do not have spatial and physical links with each other or their direct environment. Figure 2.1 presents the changes in built-up areas since 1975. The growth rate of built-up areas is twice the growth rate of the population. Dedensification and missed opportunities to coordinate new development at the city level are leading to inefficient development, increasing the costs of service provision and burdening commerce and industry with additional expenses.

Urban expansion has been encouraged by exemptions in urban planning and the absence of a legal framework to guide national and regional operations. Such a framework is needed to modernize and provide greater flexibility to urban planning rules. Subsidies on social housing construction through tax exemptions and the ad hoc mobilization of public land at low prices in the outskirts of cities have encouraged leapfrogging since the 2000s. Similarly, the New Towns Program (Programme de villes nouvelles) launched by the Ministry of Housing in 2004 (designed to provide structures and services likely to meet people's expectations regarding housing and infrastructure) also have contributed to urban dedensification and compounded the lack of connectivity infrastructure linking new town residents to jobs and economic opportunities in established centers (Ballout 2017). These policies have come at a price and generated negative externalities for cities (including Greater Casablanca, Marrakesh, and Rabat-Salé-Temara). In the Rabat agglomeration, the cost of underused infrastructure is estimated at DH 2.7 billion for the 118 kilometers

FIGURE 2.1
Growth of built-up areas in Morocco's main agglomerations

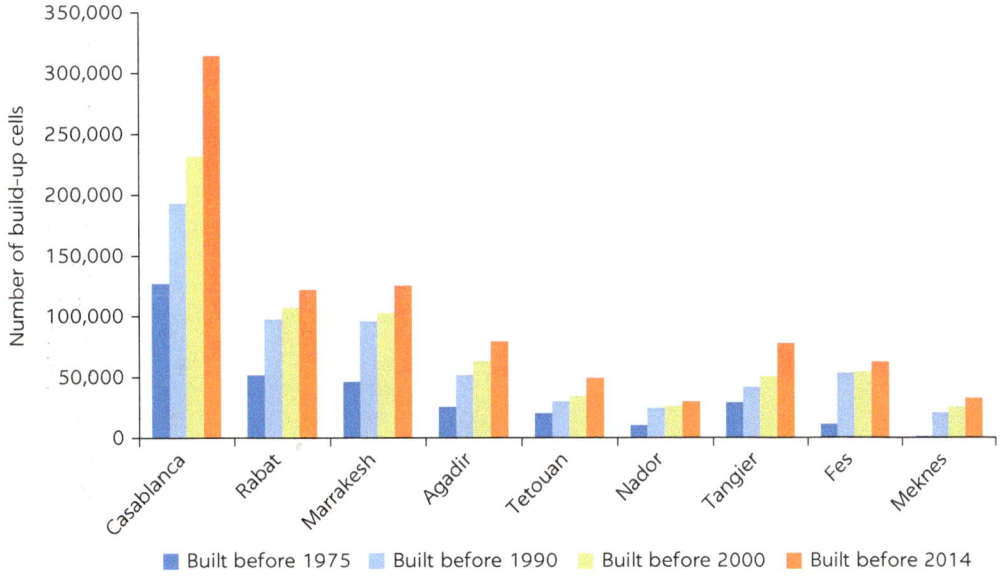

Sources: World Bank calculations based on data from Global Human Settlement Layer; Pesaresi et al. 2015.

of underused roads mostly servicing unused plots (Ministère de l'Urbanisme et de l'Aménagement du Territoire 2016).

Similarly, the creation of new neighborhoods on the fringes of cities to build social housing or rehouse slum dwellers has also exacerbated leapfrogging development (see map 2.1). Fiscal incentives are provided nationally to promote social housing. When managed well, such interventions are likely to have a positive impact, but they can be costly. For instance, the cost of subsidies for upgrading infrastructure and providing housing for slum dwellers in the Errahma area of Casablanca has been estimated at DH 1.28 billion (LYDEC 2013). Adding to these costs, leapfrogging tends to favor periurban development over redevelopment of central areas and makes public transport less attractive.

Accessing land for industrial and commercial use

The supply of public and private land and the nature of land regulation seem to be obstacles to investment in Morocco.[2] More than 40 percent of manufacturing firms identify access to land as a major hurdle for doing business, according to the World Bank's Enterprise Surveys (figure 2.2). The problem is likely much worse than this figure suggests because the Enterprise Surveys measure only the responses of firms that successfully addressed start-up constraints. In 2009, investors in Morocco waited more than three months for a building permit.

Public ownership of industrial land makes business development more complicated, detaching land supply from market demand, creating shortages, mispricing land (thus inviting speculation), and often misallocating investment in land improvements. But acquiring privately owned land is often equally problematic because of weak property rights and outdated supply-driven land use plans.

Economic costs of land misallocation

Challenges for businesses in accessing land have lowered productivity in Morocco. Recent research computes the degree of land misallocation in the Moroccan manufacturing sector and the potential productivity gain—total factor

MAP 2.1

Leapfrog urban development in Morocco: Greater Casablanca and Rabat-Salé-Temara

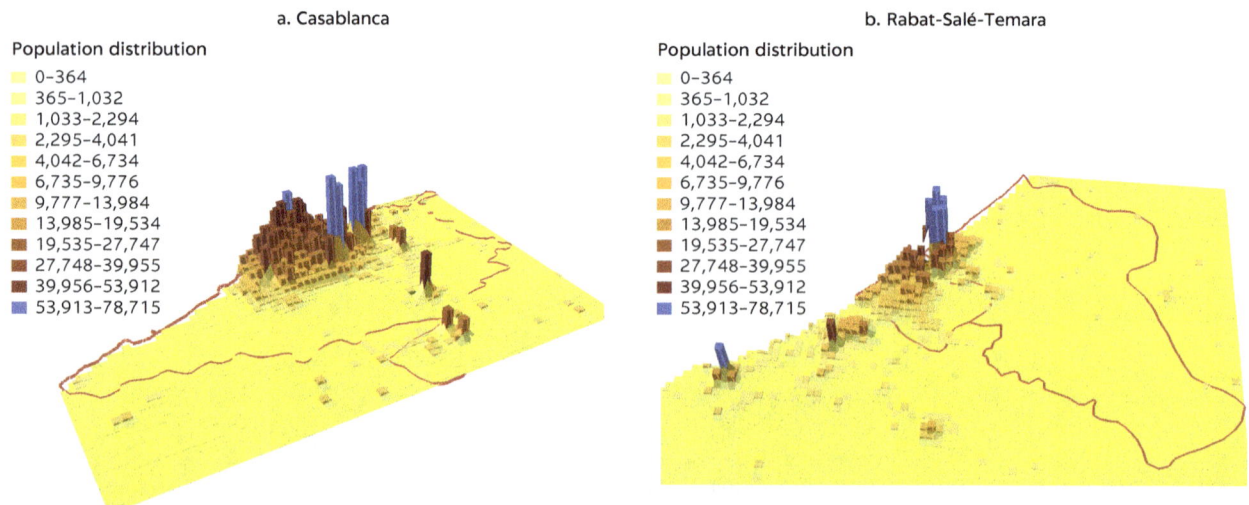

Source: World Bank using ArcScene maps with data from Landscan 2012 (Bright, Rose, and Urban 2013).

FIGURE 2.2
Perception of firms in select countries regarding access to land as a major constraint for business development

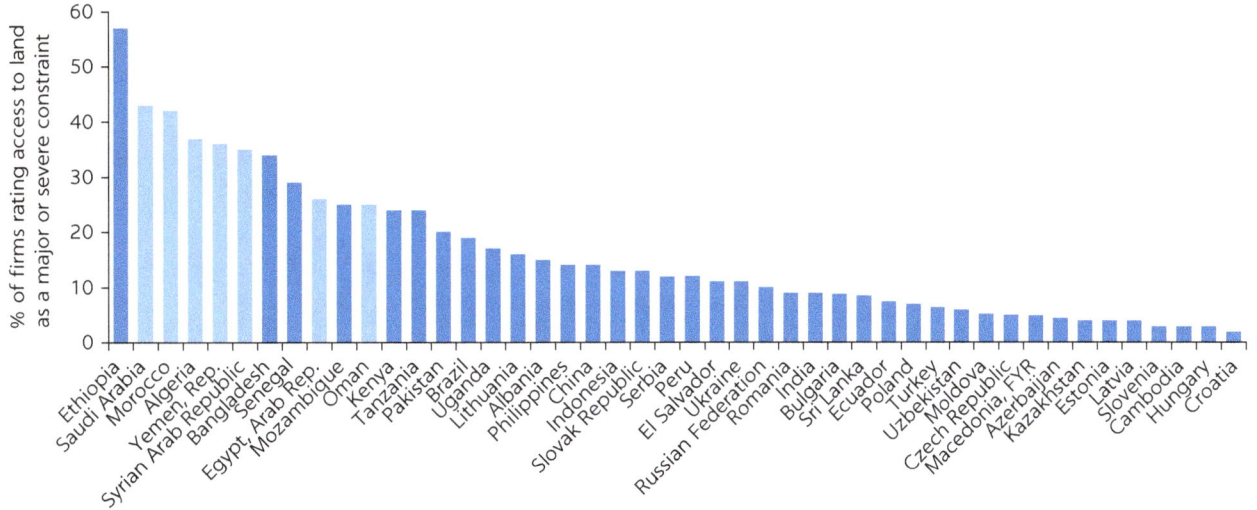

Source: World Bank 2009, based on World Bank Enterprise Surveys, various years.
Note: Only private and domestic manufacturing firms are included.

productivity (TFP)—associated with better reallocation of land across firms (Chauffour and Diaz-Sanchez 2017). The research shows that the degree of distortions in the land market is part of broader market distortions. A full removal of distortions on land markets in manufacturing would increase TFP 16 percent. In addition, better reallocation of land would raise TFP almost 11 percent.

Challenge 2: Strengthening decentralized institutions to improve service provision

As market forces support economic concentration, the key question for decision makers is whether their actions have helped to balance living standards and make development inclusive. Consider the incidence of poverty. Urban poverty rates have declined faster than the national poverty rate: in 2001, urban poverty was half the national level; in 2014, it decreased to a third. However, poverty rates in rural areas are almost twice as high as the national level. As of 2014, 40 percent of the population lived in rural areas, accounting for 79.4 percent of the 1.6 million poor and 62.1 percent of the 5.4 million vulnerable. Rural-urban disparities in poverty are large and sustained.

There are spatial disparities in access to basic services and infrastructure. While access to services tends to be higher in urban areas than in rural areas in the same region, access rates vary significantly across regions by type of area (urban or rural). While the gap in access to electricity has been reduced drastically, the gap in access to running water and to sanitation is almost 30 percentage points between urban areas in the leading and most lagging regions (see figure 2.3). The gap in access is comparable across rural areas with respect to improved sanitation services, but is significantly larger with respect to running water. Access to health services also varies significantly across regions. For example, the region of Rabat-Salé-Zemmour-Zaer is the best equipped in public

FIGURE 2.3
Access to running water and improved sanitation in Morocco, by region, 2014

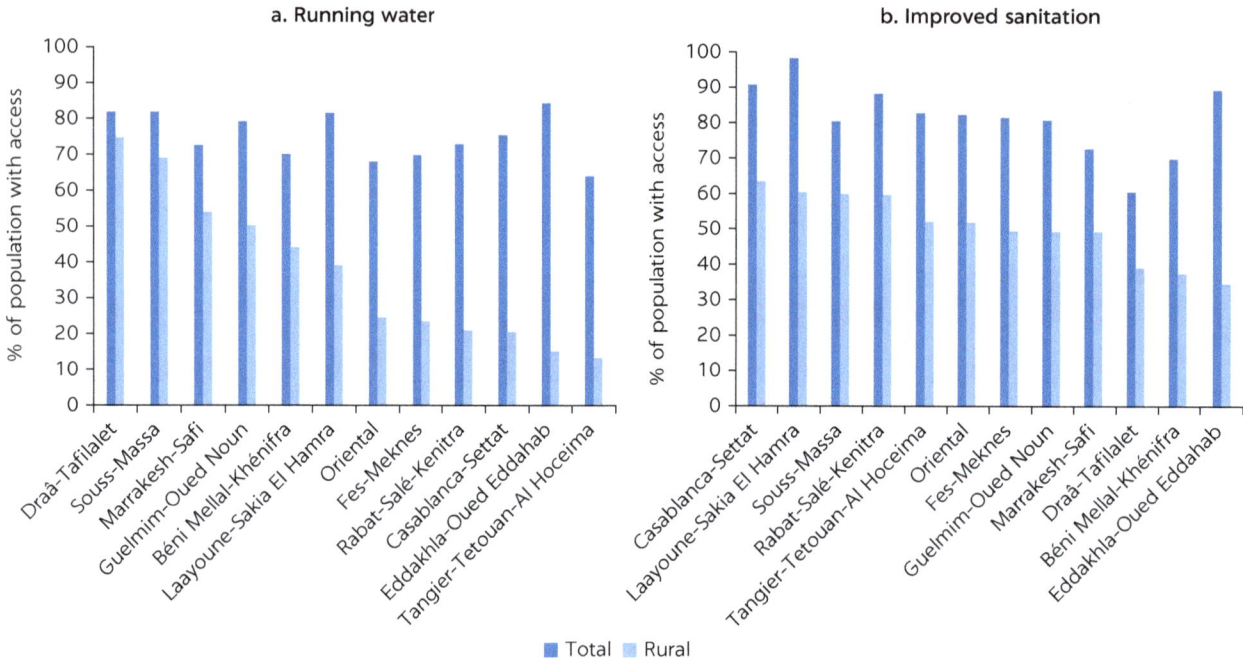

Source: World Bank calculations based on data from HCP 2014.

hospitals (15 hospitals), with 680 inhabitants per hospital bed compared with 2,121 inhabitants per hospital bed in the region of Gharb-Chrarda-Béni Hssen. A comparable variation exists in access to medical staff.[3]

The government's regionalization and decentralization agendas, if implemented effectively as outlined in the introduction to this note, can help to equip regions with resources and capacity to fulfill their mandate of spatial and economic planning. The division of responsibilities between central and local authorities provides an opportunity to fill the widening gap in service provision. This process needs to be accompanied by a deconcentration reform, which has been on standby but is essential for implementing integrated politics at different levels.

Meeting Morocco's urban development challenges requires substantial financing. The estimated investment requirements for urban infrastructure in Moroccan cities amount to around DH 320 billion over the 2017–27 period, with an estimated DH 222 billion over the decade, or DH 22.2 billion per year, to be financed by urban municipalities themselves.[4] In comparison, the total capital expenditure of urban municipalities over the 2009–15 period stagnated at around DH 4.5 billion per year, around 20 percent of the estimated annual investment required from municipalities to provide cities with the infrastructure they need to improve living standards and economic activity in their territories.

Municipalities can use several levers to increase their investment in urban infrastructure. First, they can improve their capacity to plan for and execute investments that fall under their direct responsibility. Second, they can strengthen their financial capacity by increasing revenues and leveraging this capacity through increased borrowing. Box 2.1 presents an example of how Tanzania has propelled municipal revenues by leveraging information systems.

> **BOX 2.1**
>
> ### Leveraging information systems to improve municipal revenues in Tanzania
>
> The Tanzania Strategic Cities Project supports seven cities in efforts to improve the efficiency of their own-source revenue collection by introducing an innovative Local Government Revenue Collection Information System (LGRCIS). LGRCIS is an electronic and geographic information system–based tool that supports revenue collection from multiple sources (service levies, property taxes, and business licenses).
>
> Before 2014, cities relied on manual tax assessments. Officials undertook field surveys, but the information gathered was inaccurate and limited. Many potential taxpayers were left off the rolls. The assessments were easily manipulated for personal gain, as were the payments, which utilized cumbersome paper-based processes. As a result, revenue channels only generated limited resources. Cities are caught in a vicious cycle—unable to fund their development plans and thus incapable of building the conducive environment for enhanced productivity and business that are needed to generate further revenues.
>
> The government started laying the foundations for LGRCIS in 2013. The system now allows proper identification of taxpayers and defaulters, invoicing, receipting, and bill generation. It facilitates electronic payments through a single gateway and enables reporting and analysis by geography, payer, or revenue types. LGRCIS has radically improved how taxes are collected, with gains in transparency, accountability, and customer focus. Further, the LGRCIS will be used as the enabling and integrated platform for urban planning, operation and maintenance, and cost recovery.
>
> By end fiscal year 2015, the results were remarkable. In one year, cities saw their own-source revenues increase an average of 30 percent; Mwanza saw an 80 percent increase. The increased revenue is critical in meeting shortfalls from central government transfers and is ploughed back into development projects. The initial success of the LGRCIS demonstrated its transformative potential. LGRCIS is now being scaled up countrywide, both through other World Bank operations and by the government.

Building local capacity to manage urbanization

The limited capacity of Moroccan municipalities to execute their investment budgets is a binding constraint. Municipalities often execute less than 50 percent of their investment plans, and the total accumulated surplus amounts to DH 29.5 billion. Municipalities have recently been (a) developing intermunicipal cooperation establishments (etablissements de cooperation intercommunale [ECIs]); (b) tapping the know-how and expertise of the private sector through private sector participation (PSP) or public service delegation; and (c) using the flexible institutional framework of joint-ownership companies (sociétés de développement local [SDLs]) to hire and retain the right skill sets for managing specific urban development projects. However, given the absence of a coherent institutional and legal framework, these solutions can lead to a dilution of the responsibilities of locally elected bodies, with the risk of undermining the accountability chain between citizens and local governments. Moroccan authorities should work on the long-term actions required to strengthen the effectiveness and accountability of local governments.

The legal framework for intermunicipal cooperation needs to be strengthened to help to manage cities at the right level. Urbanization in Morocco is leading to metropolization, with larger cities growing beyond their municipal boundaries. The introduction of ECIs in the 2015 Organic Law 113-14[5] was intended to provide metropolitan agglomerations with a framework for service provision at the intermunicipal level. Morocco already has several ECIs. In order to provide municipalities with the right tools, the legal and institutional framework for intermunicipal cooperation will require further development.

First, ECIs need to have a framework for financial sustainability and autonomy. The existing ECIs rely on voluntary contributions from municipalities, which are not sufficient and are too unpredictable for them to fulfill even their limited mandates. The government should develop a framework for equipping ECIs with predictable and sufficient financial resources. This framework could set rules for compensating the transferred responsibilities, earmarking specific transfers from the central government to ECIs, and allocating revenues from specific taxes to ECIs. Alternative intermunicipal funding mechanisms subject to intermunicipal cooperation, such as the contracts plan (contratos plan) in Colombia described in box 2.2, could complement the current endeavor.

Second, the responsibilities transferred to ECIs should be extended to the provision of most of the major local public and utility services, in order to ensure the coherent development of their urban agglomeration. As part of the clarification of roles and mandate for urban planning, ECIs should also take a larger role in preparing territorial plans at the level of urban agglomerations. Indeed, international experience shows that integrating land use and transport planning at the metropolitan level helps to promote the efficiency of urban growth.

Third, the government should ensure that ECIs are established at the relevant geographic scale. It would be helpful to produce a national map of ECIs, with one ECI per urban agglomeration (see the example in box 2.3).

Municipalities and ECIs need to have stronger control over the SDLs and the PSP arrangements operating in their territories. PSP and SDLs have proved to be useful tools for increasing managerial and technical capacity for the

---

BOX 2.2

"Contratos plan": An intermunicipal investment mechanism in Colombia

In order for public investment to reduce territorial gaps, articulation between the different levels of government is critical. In Colombia, political decentralization and the plurality of sources of investment financing in a context of limited subnational capacity have increased the importance of coordinating government efforts. The contratos plan or "contracts plan" is a mechanism created in the government's National Development Plan 2010–2014 as a response to the challenges in coordinating the use of public investment funds between the national and subnational governments. A contracts plan is a memorandum of understanding (acuerdo de voluntades) between the different levels of government of a department or region that includes an agreed medium-term investment program for territorial development to be cofinanced by the government of Colombia and the subnational governments involved. Based on the experiences of countries such as France, the government has piloted 7 contracts plans in 9 departments and 272 municipalities with the ultimate goal of fostering regional convergence. The pilot confirmed the potential of the tool to strengthen decentralization, improve planning, and promote regional development. However, the pilots also provided evidence that further improvements in the tool are needed, including in the definition of their scope and focus, project design, use of incentives, transparency mechanisms, and rules of operation, among others.

> **BOX 2.3**
>
> ### Rationalizing the geography of intermunicipal cooperation: A recent example in France
>
> France has a long history of intermunicipal cooperation. As in most countries, the first structures emerged as ad hoc associations of municipalities aimed at organizing the collective management of specific services. In France, this process started at the end of the 19th century with the first associations of municipalities (syndicats de communes). The model evolved after the Second World War with the development of general-purpose intermunicipal structures (communautés) promoted in large urban agglomerations. By 2010, most French municipalities belonged to one or more of the 15,636 specific-purpose syndicats and 2,393 general-purpose communautés that existed at the time.
>
> The 2010 reform of local governments (réforme des collectivités territoriales) initiated a process of rationalization of intermunicipal cooperation by launching the elaboration of a coherent territorial model (carte intercommunale) and by making it mandatory for municipalities to participate in an intermunicipal cooperation structure. The process of consolidation and rationalization was confirmed by the 2015 Law on the New Territorial Organization (Loi portant nouvelle organization territoriale de la république), which gave the governors (préfets) of each department the responsibility of implementing the law through the development of consolidated maps of intermunicipal structures in each department. In 2017, for the first time and after more than a century of intermunicipal cooperation, France now has a coherent national map of intermunicipal structures.

provision of specific services and the execution of urban development projects (see box 2.4). However, municipalities have limited control over these structures and often lack the technical capacity to manage PSP contracts adequately. The ownership structure of many SDLs often gives participating municipalities only a minority stake, and the *wali* generally presides over the board of directors and designates the chief executive officer. Above everything, the lack of technical and managerial capacity limits the ability of municipalities to exert effective control over PSP and SDLs operating in their territory. This situation limits local ownership of the policies carried out, further eroding accountability in the provision of key urban services.

Municipalities should be allowed to hire staff with the appropriate skills needed to fulfill their functions. The legal framework of local public services should be reformed to allow municipalities to hire key staff—including general managers, technical directors, and other technical staff—at attractive remuneration levels. The possibility should also be open for municipalities to hire specific staff on a contractual basis in order to fulfill specific time-bound responsibilities.

Increasing the financial capacity of municipalities

An improved municipal finance framework would allow municipalities to bridge the investment gap without the need for increased transfers from the central government. Investment in urban municipalities stagnated between DH 4 billion and DH 5 billion during the 2009–15 period. The net saving of urban municipalities amounted to around DH 2.4 billion in 2015 or 13 percent of the municipalities' recurrent revenues. The rest of municipal investment expenditure was financed by investment grants in the amount of around DH 1.5 billion and borrowing in the amount of around DH 1.2 billion.

> **BOX 2.4**
>
> ### Morocco's experience with PSP and SDLs
>
> Morocco has a long experience of delegated management of commercial services (delegation de service public) through PSP and autonomous publicly owned utilities (régies autonomes). PSP in the provision of urban infrastructure services was introduced in Morocco through the negotiation of concession contracts for the delivery of water supply, sanitation, and electricity in Casablanca (1997), Rabat (1999), and Tangier-Tetouan (2002). A specific legal framework for PSP was introduced in 2006 through Law 54-05, and PSP has developed since then, especially in the urban transport and solid waste management sectors. PSP in Morocco mostly follows the leasing (affermage) model in which the public sector retains the responsibility for financing capital investment plans.
>
> The development of PSP has contributed a great deal to improving the efficiency and quality of service delivery in the sectors in which it has been introduced. For the last five years, the role of the private sector has grown continuously. More than 100 cities have contracted private operators to provide street cleaning and waste collection services, which benefit more than 15 million people today. More recently, the model of SDLs, (of which more than 50 percent of the capital must be held by public legal entities) was introduced in the 2009 Municipal Charter, and its structure was confirmed in the 2015 Organic Law 113-14. SDLs have proved increasingly popular over the last years. In Casablanca and Rabat-Salé, SDLs have been created to develop and manage urban transport investments and parking infrastructure, but also to manage urban development projects; in Casablanca, an SDL (casa prestations) is in charge of carrying out institutional modernization missions for the municipality.

The government is not likely to be able to increase significantly the amount currently dedicated to supporting municipal investment; municipalities will therefore need to take the lead in efforts to fill the investment gap. They could do this by using all of the available levers to improve the municipal finance framework—at both the central and local levels. These levers include (a) improving the current policy on fiscal transfers, by increasing the transparency, predictability, and performance orientation of the funds transferred by the central government, (b) improving the return on taxes administered by the government on behalf of municipalities, (c) simplifying local tax regulations to achieve higher returns, and (d) leveraging higher net saving and creditworthiness to increase sustainable borrowing.

The impact of fiscal transfers can be improved through increased predictability and stronger incentives. The government currently supports municipalities by allocating them a large part of the amounts collected from the value added tax (taxe sur la valeur ajoutée). Mechanisms for the allocation and transfer of funds from the value added tax to municipalities can be strengthened by revamping the formula for allocating funds to incentivize municipalities to strengthen (a) their institutional capacity, (b) their performance in the provision of municipal services and the mobilization of their own resources, and (c) their financial sustainability and capacity to finance the required investments. Direct financial transfers to municipalities should become the default mechanism. International experience shows that intergovernmental fiscal transfers that are stable, transparent, and predictable help to lay the groundwork for long-term investment planning and give municipalities greater financial responsibility.

Improving the return on taxes administered by the government on behalf of the municipalities

The government currently administers three taxes on behalf of municipalities: (a) local service tax (taxe sur les services communaux), (b) housing tax (taxe d'habitation), and (c) business tax (taxe professionnelle). These three taxes represent about a fourth of municipal revenues, but they constitute an important untapped potential. The three taxes are based on the rental value of real estate and productive assets. The collection associated with these taxes is limited by the lack of up-to-date property registries and declared values. In addition, a very significant share of revenues is not collected (outstanding amounts for the three taxes increased from DH 10.7 billion in 2009 to DH 14.2 billion in 2013). The current outstanding amounts represent the equivalent of more than 2.5 years' worth of revenues from the same taxes. One of the main constraints to improving the revenues from these local taxes is the lack of coordination between the different agencies involved in their administration, including the municipalities, the General Directorate of Taxes (Direction Génerale des Impots), and the National Treasury (Tresorerie Generale du Royaume). A reform of the administration of these taxes should aim to (a) expand the tax base through improved addressing and improved registration of taxable properties, (b) give greater autonomy to municipalities to determine the tax rate in their territory, and (c) improve the coordination and exchange of information between the agencies involved in administering these taxes, including through the concentration of responsibilities in one agency.

Municipalities can significantly increase their own-source revenues. The collection rate of local taxes and fees is between one-third and half of the fiscal potential in most Moroccan cities. Revenues from local taxes administered by municipalities could be increased significantly by improving the tax base and increasing the collection levels. This task would be facilitated by simplifying and consolidating the large number of existing local taxes. Local tax administration services should be strengthened by recruiting qualified agents and providing them with incentives similar to the ones provided to agents in the central tax administration. Information technology (IT) systems should also be modernized. In addition, municipalities will need the support of the relevant government agencies, including the deconcentrated authorities of the state (under the *walis* and governors) and the National Treasury, which is responsible for the legal pursuit of unpaid taxes.

Leveraging increased net saving and creditworthiness for increased and sustainable borrowing

Strengthening the financial capacity of Moroccan municipalities would directly improve their capacity to bridge the investment gap in urban infrastructure. The level of indebtedness of Moroccan municipalities is relatively low, both compared with their peers abroad as well as compared with the current moderate level of their net savings. Moroccan municipalities could use borrowing to raise their investment level. As an example, a simulation carried out for Casablanca illustrates how higher revenues could affect the municipality's investment capacity. By boosting revenues from taxes and other fees by 5 percent a year, while simultaneously maintaining a 2 percent annual increase in all other expenditure and revenue items, Casablanca could increase its savings almost fivefold over a period of six years. The city could thus fully self-finance DH 2.7 billion of investments. It also could borrow more while maintaining its ratio of debt to gross savings at its current level of 4. The investments could then amount to DH 4.8 billion over the period. By gradually increasing its debt-to-income ratio to 6, the city could invest DH 6.2 billion over the period.

INFRASTRUCTURE NEEDS IN CITIES AND REGIONS: WHAT'S NEXT?

One of the key drivers of markets and government policy is the set of challenges associated with connectivity. Restrictions on mobility can reduce the productivity of people in certain places, and it can raise costs, thus lowering living standards, especially for the poor and vulnerable for whom connectivity costs often reflect a high share of their income.

Challenge 1: Invest in smart urban mass transport to lower urban congestion costs and link people to jobs

Many Moroccan cities are confronted with high and increasing traffic congestion that imposes a cost on citizens and government. Forecasts predict that the road network in many major cities in Morocco could reach saturation soon. In Casablanca, for example, more than half of the city's main intersections are regularly heavily congested. Congestion in Casablanca is estimated to cost the nation US$300 million per year. In addition, it contributes to air pollution and adversely affects the health and well-being of the population. The annual cost of air pollution is estimated at roughly US$730 million per year, with roughly half attributed to Casablanca.[6] Table 2.1 presents the average commercial speed of

TABLE 2.1 **Average commercial speed of buses in Morocco's largest agglomerations**

URBAN AGGLOMERATION	COMMERCIAL SPEED (KILOMETERS PER HOUR)
Morocco	
Rabat	19
Agadir	18
Marrakesh	16
Fes	16
Tangier	15
Casablanca	13
OECD countries	
Copenhagen	21
Warsaw	21
Berlin	19
Vienna	19
Paris	17
Lisbon	17

Source: World Bank based on data from Morocco Ministry of Interior and the International Road and Transport Union.
Note: OECD = Organisation for Economic Co-operation and Development.

buses in cities in Morocco and in select Organisation for Economic Co-operation and Development (OECD) countries, showing the differential impact of congestion on the time needed to move people and goods.

The demographic trends that have contributed to greater congestion are projected to continue. Changes in societal norms regarding autonomy, markets, and government efforts to expand access to vehicles (access to cheaper cars and cheaper car financing) and inefficiency of public transport alternatives have contributed to a rise in the number of registered vehicles in Morocco. The number of registered vehicles in Morocco rose 70 percent in the past decade to more than 3.6 million vehicles. While the growth in registered vehicles over the past decade was high, the motorization rate remains relatively low in Morocco compared with other countries, especially OECD countries, which may signal the potential for significant growth. The motorization rate in Morocco varies significantly by region, with the regions containing Casablanca and Rabat accounting for roughly half of the vehicles (and only about 20 percent of the population). Although the share of vehicles in other regions is relatively low, annual motorization growth rates are high in most cases and stand at about 7 percent per year.

Unmet demand for urban public transit

Urban public transit demand exceeds supply in many cities in Morocco, costing people and the economy time. Buses are too few in number in many cities (relative to comparator cities), which increases the amount of time it takes to move people, while simultaneously deteriorating the conditions under which people are moving. The urban sprawl described previously in this report contributes to the rise in travel distances, which increases pressure on a public transit system already strained in many agglomerations in Morocco.

Cost of public transit

The cost to the user of public transit can be high and has a significant impact on the poor, placing them at a further disadvantage. Poor households are limited in the modes of transportation they can access because vehicle ownership is out of reach for many of them, as are tram tickets in Casablanca and Rabat. Informal transport providers operate in parallel to registered bus lines without integrated ticket and schedule systems, further increasing the commute time and cost for residents in poorer semiurban areas (especially large slums). Women, youth, the elderly, and people with reduced mobility feel the adverse effects the most. Urban transport costs some poor households up to 20 percent of their incomes.

While fragmented urban expansion and inefficient public transit limit the spatial match of jobs and employees, surveys have found them to have a larger negative impact on low-income youth. The distance between places where lower-income youth reside and where employment is located, as well as the lack of public transit, are factors contributing to the high youth unemployment rate in Morocco. A daily commute can cost disadvantaged youth a fourth to a third of their daily earnings. Many entry-level jobs require employees to work evenings and weekends, when public transportation is not available or is less frequently available, making those jobs out of reach for many young people.

Urban connectivity challenges, poor financial health of local governments, and limited ability to manage urban transit effectively

Congestion, insufficient supply of public transit, and the relatively high cost associated with it are linked with the financial health of the sector. The Ministry of Interior estimates that, to improve the level of transportation service around the nation, Morocco needs US$3 billion in investments over the next decade. Historically, though, expenditures on urban transport at the local level have represented approximately one-third of the investments required to meet the demands of residents. Further, significant annual deficits are related to public transport, and in 2014 the annual deficit in Casablanca and Rabat amounted to approximately US$30 million. Historically, public transit revenues have covered a small share of operating costs for several reasons, including substantial personnel costs associated with historic overstaffing and high maintenance and fuel costs associated with aging fleets (for example, the average age of Casablanca's bus fleet is 15 years). Further, cities have limited financial resources to dedicate to urban transit because of limitations in their taxing capacity and in their ability to borrow.

These challenges are also associated with limitations in local governments' ability to manage urban transit effectively. Moroccan cities are constrained in their ability to coordinate land use and transportation plans, especially across municipal boundaries. In most cities in Morocco, Urban Mobility Plans (Plans de déplacement urbain [PDUs]) and Urban Development Master Plans (Schémas directeurs d'aménagement urbain [SDAUs]) are developed independently and occasionally even contradict one another. However, without an integrated territorial perspective, sectoral strategies might entail additional costs in urbanization and even exacerbate territorial disparities. For example, in Casablanca, the most recent Urban Mobility Plan was completed prior to the development of a new Land Use Plan; as a result, the city was forced to update it at great cost after a few years. To prevent such situations and demonstrate its willingness to improve interministerial relations concerning urban subjects, the government established a ministry in charge of urban policy. Furthermore, cities are constrained in their ability to achieve network synergies or economies of scale in urban transport in part because the necessary institutional arrangements for intermunicipal cooperation have not yet been widely adopted or made functional, with a few exceptions.

Challenge 2: Strengthen logistics management to reduce regional market fragmentation

In Morocco, like in many other countries, physical connectivity declines with distance from the coast. The vast majority of the population lives near the coast and in areas with relatively high access to cities of greater than 50,000 inhabitants. Nevertheless, a portion of the population lives in interior areas with relatively intermediate access to cities of 50,000 or more inhabitants (see map 2.2, which illustrates the decline in physical connectivity toward the interior of the Northeast region of the country). Thus, the government of Morocco, like other governments, must make connectivity investments both to increase efficiency and to address equity considerations. Despite significant progress made under the National Strategy for the Enhancement of Logistics Competitiveness 2010–2015 (Stratégie nationale pour le développement de la compétitivité logistique 2010–2015), an evaluation conducted by the Moroccan

MAP 2.2
Physical connectivity for households in relatively sparsely populated regions of Morocco: The case of the Northeast region

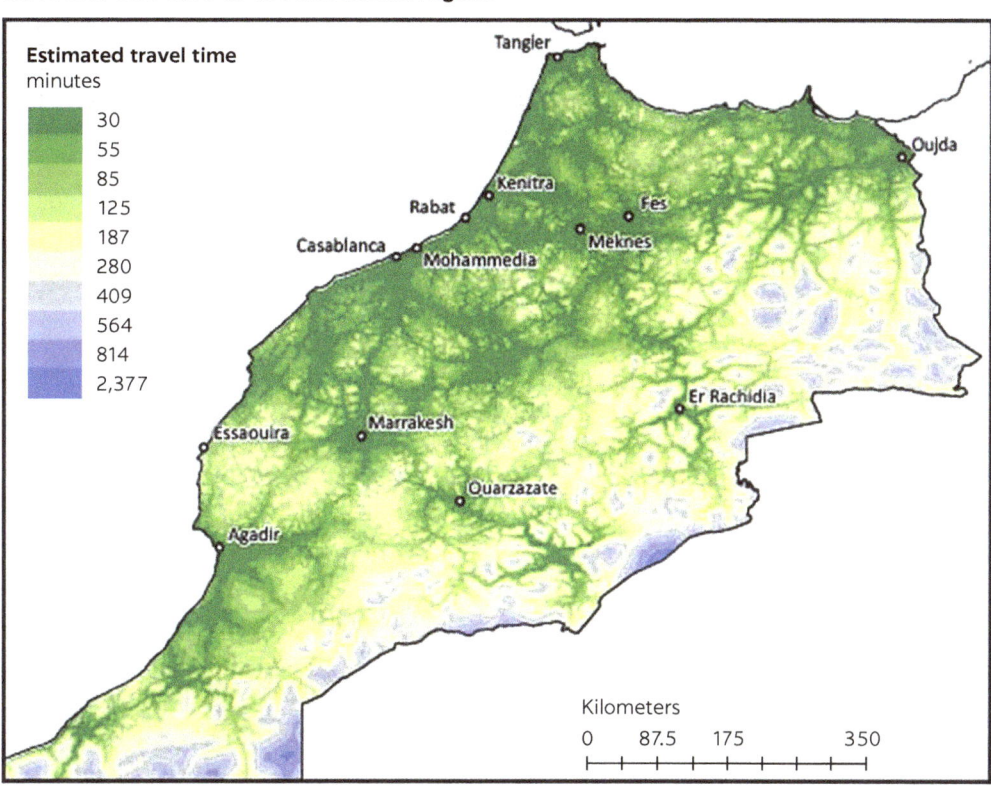

Source: World Bank based on Weiss et al. 2018.

Agency for the Development of Logistics (Agence Marocaine de Développement de la Logistique) highlights the need to implement an ambitious action plan to strengthen the achievements made so far, especially in terms of connectivity.

Elevated domestic transport costs

The cost of transporting goods across Morocco amounts to roughly 17 percent of merchandise values compared with 7 percent in neighboring countries. This high cost is driven in part by the atomization and poor quality of freight. Approximately 90 percent of freight operators own just one or two trucks. Most freight operators—roughly 70–75 percent—are informal. The supply of specialized vehicles, such as refrigerated trucks, does not meet demand. Furthermore, the fleet is antiquated, with an average age of 13 years for freight vehicles.

Connectivity in significantly rural regions—those that could be characterized as relatively lagging regions—is also constrained compared with connectivity in other countries in the region. Low rural connectivity disadvantages people living in predominantly rural regions. In a recent analysis of rural access indexes, Morocco scored 36 percent relative to a Middle East and North Africa average of 58 percent.

Information connectivity

National information and communication technology connectivity is positively correlated with growth, job creation, and innovation; despite recent gains, access is low in Morocco relative to other countries in the region.

Fixed broadband penetration as a percentage of households and mobile broadband penetration as a percentage of the population in Middle East and North African countries are, on average, more than twice the penetration rates in Morocco (figure 2.4).

Spatial inequalities in access to broadband are significant. Access rates are significantly lower in secondary cities of the country than in the main cities, even where population sizes are similar. Internet access is lower in rural areas than in urban areas, although the access gap has been closing faster in rural areas more recently. The national digital strategy—Maroc Digital 2020—defined in 2017 seeks to address this challenge, aiming to reduce the digital gap by 50 percent.

FIGURE 2.4

Fixed and mobile broadband penetration in Morocco and select Middle East and North African countries, 2015

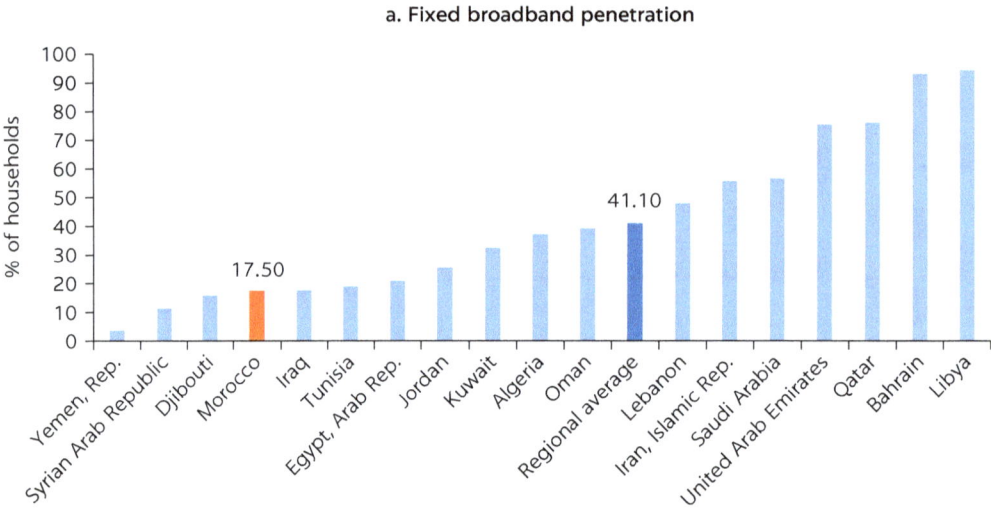

a. Fixed broadband penetration

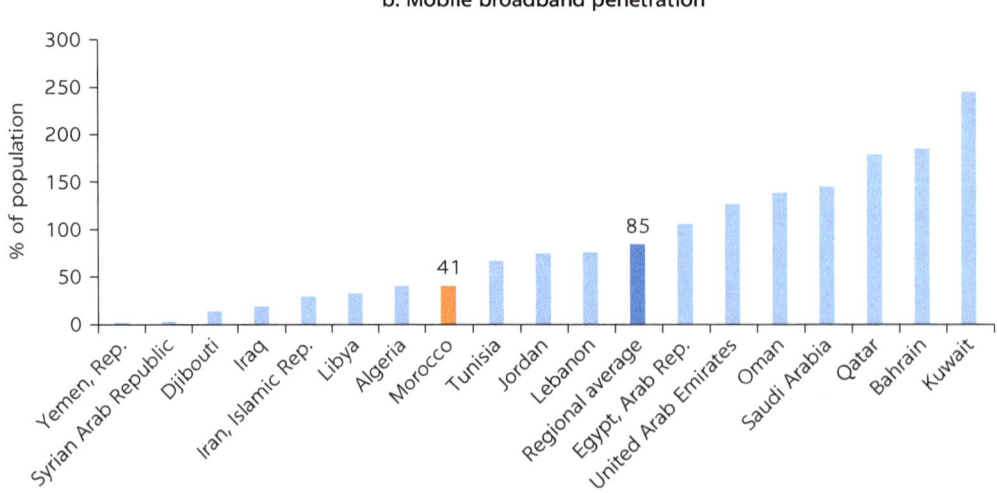

b. Mobile broadband penetration

Source: TeleGeography's GlobalComms Database for 2015.
Note: Fixed broadband includes mainly ADSL and, to a lesser extent, optic fiber. Mobile broadband includes mobile Internet plans (3G and 4G) for data only as well as for voice and data.

Challenge 3: Interventions to increase opportunities for young Moroccan women and men

Integration of young Moroccans into the labor market is one of the major challenges for policy makers. Young people ages 15–29 account for about 30 percent of Morocco's population and 44 percent of the working-age population. Despite positive rates of economic growth over the previous decade, averaging 4.3 percent annually, Morocco's youth have been affected disproportionately by economic exclusion. The Moroccan economy has created a net of only 87,500 jobs per year, on average, not nearly enough to absorb the estimated 224,000 new labor market entrants—including 148,000 youth—each year. Overall, there are more than 1 million unemployed job seekers in Morocco, 70 percent of whom are ages 15–29 years, while up to 3.5 million youth in the same age group are currently not in education, employment, or training, the majority of whom live in cities.

There is a growing need to improve the socioeconomic status of Morocco's next generations by providing more opportunities to participate in political or social decision-making processes in cities. The correlation between youth unemployment, social exclusion, and the risk for social and political instability is substantial. Youth hold potential in both economic and social spheres: it is important that urban development strategies and programs promote civil participation, especially among youth. In this sense, cities are places where youth should feel like true stakeholders. Morocco's municipalities need to view youth as future leaders within cities and communities and as essential to innovation and sustainable growth.

Inclusion of youth and women in urban development is a critical factor for spatial planning and can be increased in innovative ways. Establishing a link between land use and accessibility becomes important to create spaces where young people can contribute to the prosperity of cities, especially young women, who face significantly more challenges than young men. By applying a framework for youths to transition through different stages of their life cycle, municipalities can improve their provision of basic services tailored to the needs of the youth population, including health services, education, and recreation. Subsequently they need to focus on access to employment and entrepreneurship, as youths reach working age. To this end, providing access to quality education with a relevant focus on the job market throughout the entire education process is essential to ensuring a smooth transition from student life to work life.

Moroccan youths lack adequate skills and information regarding economic opportunities. There is a significant skills gap for semiqualified technicians and operators, and there is a strong need for semiqualified workers with no secondary school diploma, especially in high-growth and key economic sectors (tourism, logistics, automotive, retail, IT, business process outsourcing, and construction). Recent studies indicate that labor demand and employment growth in Morocco (currently at about 90,000 jobs per year) could be higher if employers were able to fill the many vacancies that exist due to lack of candidates with adequate technical, language, behavioral, and IT skills.

The challenges facing young women are particularly high, and very few employers are considering effective means to support a gender-balanced workforce. For these reasons, achieving gender equality is another major challenge for Morocco. In 2015, the country had some 2.7 million economically inactive young people ages 15–29 (including young women). With less than one-quarter of working-age women active (in the labor market), Morocco is among the world's lowest 20 percent of countries for female labor market participation (World Bank 2013). Moroccan women still suffer many inequalities regarding access to employment as well as legal discrimination. For instance, women lag behind in terms of rights to economic assets (inheritance), social security benefits, and marital property (World Bank 2015). Along with the integration of youth into the labor market, the authorities should also improve access to economic opportunities for women, promote their empowerment, increase their emancipation, and mainstream gender equality into public policies.

Successful interventions depend on the capacity of city decision makers to coordinate with different levels of government and the private sector through coalitions of public and private players and to foster interventions across four broad policy levers. These levers are strongly intertwined and together provide a comprehensive framework for assessing the policy options that city leaders can deploy to foster economic growth, create jobs, increase productivity, and attract investment. Table 2.2 illustrates the interventions that the national government, city leaders, and private sector could deploy in each of the policy levers to promote the creation of more and better jobs for youths.

International experience shows that local policies can help to bridge the skills gap. For example, the city of Coimbatore in India has been able to sustain rapid growth and job creation in the manufacturing and industrial sector thanks to its thriving collection of vocational training institutions. This directed training is achieved efficiently through the private sector's involvement in devising curricula and sponsoring internships and through the participation of universities or university departments. In the city of Changsha in China, the government led the improvement of vocational training programs by stimulating

TABLE 2.2 **Policy interventions to promote competitive cities in Morocco**

LEVEL OF INTERVENTION	INSTITUTIONS AND REGULATIONS	INFRASTRUCTURE AND LAND	SKILLS AND INNOVATION	ENTERPRISE SUPPORT AND FINANCE
National government	Macroeconomic management; national investment and trade policy; legal framework and property protection; industry-specific taxes and regulations	Highways, roads, airports, and ports; power grid; regulations for infrastructure provision, such as public-private partnership laws	Public education system; immigration policies to attract talent; research and development funding support schemes; health care	Export and trade facilitation; access to finance support schemes
City government	Municipal taxes and incentives; zoning and land use policies; construction permits; business licenses; public safety and law enforcement	City roads and public transportation; water and sanitation; public safety; housing and slum upgrading	Talent attraction programs; cluster development support; linking firms with academia	Business support services; investment policies, promotion, and aftercare; facilitation of seed, catalyst, and risk capital
Private sector	Standards and certification associations	Additional infrastructure and shared services	Vocational training programs; research and development	Business associations and support networks; market intelligence and business information; equity and debt

Source: World Bank 2015.

competition among schools and strengthening the links between schools and businesses. The government provided funding to schools on the basis of enrollment numbers, and it offered tax credits to firms for sending participants to worker training programs. Performance data on vocational training were distributed among businesses. Funding was provided for training offices as well as for fairs and exhibitions.

The next chapter of this note summarizes the challenges facing Morocco with regard to leveraging urbanization for economic growth and shared prosperity and describes targeted interventions and priority reforms to address them.

NOTES

1. On April 19, 2017, as part of a plenary session of the Houses of Parliament devoted to presentation of the government program, the head of government, Saad Eddin El Othmani, announced that the government aims to implement a comprehensive reform of the land sector in order to promote its governance and facilitate its mobilization for investment projects.
2. This section is an extract from Benhassine et al. (2009).
3. The two panels show that access to services in rural areas of regions with large demographic and economic centers, such as Casablanca, Rabat, and Tangier, is lower than access in regions that are less attractive economically. An explanation could be that many periurban villages in dynamic regions, which are considered rural, suffer from their proximity to large agglomerations because they grow rapidly, while access to services improves more slowly.
4. These estimations are based on work carried out as part of the urbanization review. The estimations are focused on infrastructure whose provision falls within the municipalities' jurisdiction, including urban roads, public spaces, sanitation, solid waste, public lighting, public buildings, and economic infrastructure. The estimates consist of extrapolations based on available plans, studies, and technical standards; they update similar estimates prepared in 2009 for the Ministry of Interior. The detailed estimates will be presented to and consulted with the authorities as part of the second phase of the urbanization review.
5. Succeeding the agglomeration groups (groupements d'agglomération) introduced by the Municipal Charter of 2009.
6. While significant, this amount is substantially lower than that of countries with major pollution problems and has been declining as a result of recent government efforts to reduce air pollution, including improving the quality standards of transport fuels (for example, restricting lead content and reducing maximum sulfur content).

REFERENCES

Ballout, Jean-Marie. 2017. "Un bilan intermédiaire du programme de villes nouvelles au Maroc." *Les Cahiers d'EMAM* [online] 29 http://emam.revues.org/1316.

Benhassine, Najy, Youssef Saadani Hassani, Philip E. Keefer, Andrew H. W. Stone, and Sameh Naguib Wahba. 2009. *From Privilege to Competition: Unlocking Private-led Growth in the Middle East and North Africa*. MENA Development Report. Washington, DC: World Bank. http://documents.worldbank.org/curated/en/144601468276305506/From-privilege-to-competition-unlocking-private-led-growth-in-the-Middle-East-and-North-Africa.

Bright, E.A., A.N. Rose, and M.L. Urban. 2013. LandScan 2012. Oak Ridge, TN: Oak Ridge National Laboratory.

Chauffour, Jean-Pierre, and Jose Luis Diaz-Sanchez. 2017. "Product and Factor Market Distortions: The Case of the Manufacturing Sector in Morocco." Policy Research Working Paper 8218, World Bank, Washington, DC.

HCP (Haut Commissariat au Plan). 2014. "Recensement général de la population et de l'habitat." HCP, Rabat. https://rgph2014.hcp.ma/.

LYDEC (Lyonnaise des Eaux de Casablanca). 2013. "Evaluation du coût complet de mise en œuvre des schémas directeurs: Mise au jour des surcoûts liés à l'équipement en eau potable et assainissement des zones d'extension du Grand Casablanca." LYDEC, Casablanca.

Ministère de l'Urbanisme et de l'Aménagement du Territoire, Morocco. 2016. "SDAU 2040, Rabat-Salé-Témara et sa zone périphérique: Analyse territorial." Ministère de l'Urbanisme et de l'Aménagement du Territoire.

Pesaresi, Martino, Daniele Ehrilch, Aneta J. Florczyk, Sergio Freire, Andreea Julea, Thomas Kemper, Pierre Soille, and Vasileios Syrris. 2015. "GHS Built-up Grid, Derived from Landsat, Multitemporal (1975, 1990, 2000, 2014)." European Commission, Joint Research Centre (dataset). http://data.europa.eu/89h/jrc-ghsl-ghs_built_ldsmt_globe_r2015b.

Weiss, D. J., A. Nelson, H. S. Gibson, W. Temperley, S. Peedell, A. Lieber, M. Hancher, E. Poyart, S. Belchior, N. Fullman, B. Mappin, U. Dalrymple, J. Rozier, T. C. D. Lucas, R. E. Howes, L. S. Tusting, S. Y. Kang, E. Cameron, D. Bisanzio, K. E. Battle, S. Bhatt, and P. W. Gething. 2018. "A Global Map of Travel Time to Cities to Assess Inequalities in Accessibility in 2015." Nature, 553(7688), 333–36. https://doi.org/10.1038/nature25181.

World Bank. 2008. "Marchés fonciers pour la croissance économique au Maroc." World Bank, Washington, DC.

———. 2009. *From Privilege to Competition: Unlocking Private-Led Growth in the Middle East and North Africa*. MENA Development Report. Washington, DC., World Bank. https://openknowledge.worldbank.org/handle/10986/13524.

———. 2013. World Development Indicators. Washington, DC: World Bank.

———. 2015. "Maroc: Équilibrer les chances-renforcer l'autonomisation des femmes pour une société plus ouverte, inclusive et prospère." Rapport 97778, World Bank, Washington, DC.

3 Conclusion

MOROCCO: THREE SERIES OF DEVELOPMENT CHALLENGES TO OVERCOME FOR BETTER ECONOMIC AND SOCIAL INCLUSION

Although Moroccan cities are engines of demographic and economic growth, urbanization has not generated the same growth benefits in Morocco as it has in countries with a similar context. Among other factors, Morocco does not sufficiently leverage agglomeration economies to enable harmonious urbanization.

Morocco faces three main challenges in promoting economic and social inclusion. These challenges are related to the three key drivers of integrated territorial development identified in the 2009 *World Development Report* (WDR) (World Bank 2009). These drivers are the "three Ds"—density, distance, and division—that are underlying agglomeration economies: (a) build population and economic density to create economies of scale for firms; (b) reduce distances through better connectivity (road and highway infrastructure and information and communication technologies) to improve access to the labor market; and (c) reduce territorial divisions (not only customs barriers, but also sociospatial and socioeconomic divisions likely to limit access to labor and land markets).

Specific challenges that constrain Morocco's ability to leverage urbanization for economic growth and shared prosperity are closely related to the three Ds. First, constraints linked to land administration (insufficient land that is affordable and developed and difficulties in accessing land for low-income households and small firms), urban and territorial land planning, and the financing and provision of basic services by territorial authorities limit the pace and efficiency of Morocco's urbanization process by contributing to trends such as urban sprawl. Second, several factors limit the circulation of people, goods, and ideas within cities (lack of connectivity, since urban growth is absorbed mainly by the cities' peripheries) as well as between cities and between regions (high cost of transport of goods). The suboptimal connectivity limits labor market effectiveness, potential for innovation, and productivity of Moroccan cities. Third, the persistence of pockets of poverty, both in urban and in rural areas, and the rise of youth employment call for interventions that target social exclusion and access to the labor market.

A FAVORABLE CONTEXT FOR COORDINATED REFORMS AT DIFFERENT LEVELS

Ongoing reforms introduced by the 2011 Constitution represent a unique opportunity for Morocco to proceed in a more relevant and effective way with the definition and implementation of integrated policies at different levels. Morocco has embarked on an ambitious agenda of institutional reform aimed at deepening decentralization (through the Advanced Regionalization laws) and deconcentration (through the Deconcentration Charter): this background should be conducive, on the one hand, to better coordination of public interventions between central and decentralized levels (promoting intersectorality) and, on the other, to the consolidation of public policies, including at regional and intermunicipal levels (which are critical levels to increase agglomeration benefits and to promote redistributive interventions targeting lagging territories).

Recently elected regional councils have a key role to play in ensuring the coordination and articulation of sectoral policies in their territories. The reforms of the Advanced Regionalization agenda widened the jurisdiction of regions to include the development and socioeconomic inclusion of their populations. The prerogatives incumbent on regions in the areas of social development and employment and vocational training place regions at the forefront of the formulation and implementation of targeted interventions for vulnerable people, such as unemployed youth. Regions also have a key role to play in developing connective infrastructure to identify and build regional and interregional transport corridors.

The central government has a key role to play in supporting and operating institutional reforms to clarify the rules of the game, to give more autonomy to local governments (in particular, municipalities and regions), to deconcentrate decision-making authority, and to provide private and public stakeholders with the right incentives. It also has a determining role to play in supporting long-term reforms aimed at improving urban management, design, and connectivity (by regulating the goods transport industry to limit its atomization and by investing in specific interregional corridors) and reducing sociospatial disparities between and within urban areas.

THREE TYPES OF TARGETED PUBLIC INTERVENTIONS AND PRIORITY REFORMS

In this promising environment, three types of public interventions would increase the potential growth benefits of urbanization for Morocco, based on three possible categories of response (the three "Is"—institutions, infrastructures, and targeted interventions), as identified in WDR 2009. According to the WDR, the factors underlying optimal urbanization processes happen at three levels: (a) institutions, which are essential to encouraging urban density through better urban development and local governance (improvement of land administration and access to appropriate basic services); (b) infrastructure, which is crucial to improving connectivity at different levels: interregional, intercity, but also intraurban (road construction and maintenance and urban transport management); and (c) targeted interventions, which are needed to address issues in the most lagging areas (underserved neighborhoods at the city level and targeted policies to reduce territorial disparities at the national level).

In line with the "three Is," there are three priority areas for action:

1. *Better prepare cities to benefit from agglomeration by giving municipalities the means to manage urban development better.* Improved management is the first major challenge for Morocco. Strengthening municipalities both financially and institutionally and improving local governance are key to addressing constraints in financing and access to land and basic services and to promoting more efficient urbanization in economic and social terms.
2. *Maximize the impact of major infrastructure on development by focusing on economic opportunities and job creation in lagging regions.* Improving connectivity within cities will require coordinated action by the government at local and national levels and greater multistakeholder consultation to implement strategic actions in close relation with territorial and urban planning.
3. *Pursue efforts to reduce sociospatial disparities, with a focus on vulnerable groups, rural economic development, and lagging regions.*

This analytical framework identifies the following priority areas for reform:

1. *Improve city financing.* Given that the financial contribution of the central government to local infrastructure is unlikely to increase, it is necessary to prioritize actions likely to strengthen the resources themselves without significantly changing the current framework for city financing. These actions should aim to enhance the efficiency of public expenditures by using government transfers at lower constant overall costs and by improving the return on municipal resources, which is very low today.
2. *Reform the implementation and governance of urban planning and urban development.* The system of regulation and implementation of urban development is currently inadequate. Its impact on urban dynamics and urban form in Morocco appears to be counterproductive, especially with regard to urban sprawl, informal housing, and the disconnect between jobs and people. It is thus urgent to develop innovative responses (such as new tools and rules of the game, new regulations, and new stakeholders), to overcome current strains, and to build a better future for urbanization. There is also a need to elaborate a national vision for cities and territories as a frame of reference, as this is a precondition for the implementation of integrated, complementary, phased, and coordinated reforms.
3. *Address spatial disparities, focusing on the importance of adapting interventions to the needs and potential of territories.* Addressing spatial disparities is needed to transform the regionalization reform agenda into a catalyst for more efficient local economic development; to strengthen relationships between different adjacent territories in terms of economic activities and territorial development by setting up development corridors; and to promote interventions that focus on increasing the income of people living in areas of persistent poverty.

Urbanization and spatial equity are not competing objectives when urbanization is supported and managed well. Too often, the concentration of people and economic activities, which characterizes all urbanization processes around the world, is seen as conflicting with the objective of balanced regional development. However, international evidence shows that urbanization and economic development go hand in hand. The recommendations offered in this note are intended to improve Morocco's ability to harness urbanization for economic development.

REFERENCE

World Bank. 2009. *World Development Report 2009: Reshaping Economic Geography.* Washington, DC: World Bank.

www.ingramcontent.com/pod-product-compliance
Lightning Source LLC
Chambersburg PA
CBHW060317240426
43661CB00059B/2796